Kateryna Zarembo, Michèle Knodt, and Maksym Yakovlyev (eds.)

TEACHING IR IN WARTIME
Experiences of University Lecturers during Russia's Full-Scale Invasion of Ukraine

Bibliografische Information der Deutschen Nationalbibliothek
Die Deutsche Nationalbibliothek verzeichnet diese Publikation in der Deutschen Nationalbibliografie; detaillierte bibliografische Daten sind im Internet über http://dnb.d-nb.de abrufbar.

Bibliographic information published by the Deutsche Nationalbibliothek
The Deutsche Nationalbibliothek lists this publication in the Deutsche Nationalbibliografie; detailed bibliographic data are available on the Internet at http://dnb.d-nb.de.

Cover photo: ID 277496318 © Svetlanashekera | Dreamstime.com

Kharkiv, Ukraine—May, 04, 2023: A university lecturer and professor walks through an auditorium destroyed by a Russian missile strike. Destruction and losses during the Russian-Ukrainian war 2022-2023. The walls in the building are destroyed, there are no windows, there are fragments of walls on the desks

ISBN (Print): 978-3-8382-1954-7
ISBN (E-Book [PDF]): 978-3-8382-7954-1
© *ibidem*-Verlag, Hannover • Stuttgart 2025

Leuschnerstraße 40
30457 Hannover
Germany / Deutschland
info@ibidem.eu

Alle Rechte vorbehalten

Das Werk einschließlich aller seiner Teile ist urheberrechtlich geschützt. Jede Verwertung außerhalb der engen Grenzen des Urheberrechtsgesetzes ist ohne Zustimmung des Verlages unzulässig und strafbar. Dies gilt insbesondere für Vervielfältigungen, Übersetzungen, Mikroverfilmungen und elektronische Speicherformen sowie die Einspeicherung und Verarbeitung in elektronischen Systemen.

All rights reserved. No part of this publication may be reproduced, stored in or introduced into a retrieval system, or transmitted, in any form, or by any means (electronic, mechanical, photocopying, recording or otherwise) without the prior written permission of the publisher. Any person who commits any unauthorized act in relation to this publication may be liable to criminal prosecution and civil claims for damages.

Printed in the EU

Soviet and Post-Soviet Politics and Society (SPPS) Vol. 281
ISSN 1614-3515

General Editor: Andreas Umland,
Stockholm Centre for Eastern European Studies, andreas.umland@ui.se

Commissioning Editor: Max Jakob Horstmann,
London, mjh@ibidem.eu

EDITORIAL COMMITTEE*

DOMESTIC & COMPARATIVE POLITICS
Prof. **Ellen Bos**, *Andrássy University of Budapest*
Dr. **Gergana Dimova**, *Florida State University*
Prof. **Heiko Pleines**, *University of Bremen*
Dr. **Sarah Whitmore**, *Oxford Brookes University*
Dr. **Harald Wydra**, *University of Cambridge*

SOCIETY, CLASS & ETHNICITY
Col. **David Glantz**, *"Journal of Slavic Military Studies"*
Dr. **Marlène Laruelle**, *George Washington University*
Dr. **Stephen Shulman**, *Southern Illinois University*
Prof. **Stefan Troebst**, *University of Leipzig*

POLITICAL ECONOMY & PUBLIC POLICY
Prof. **Andreas Goldthau**, *University of Erfurt*
Dr. **Robert Kravchuk**, *University of North Carolina*
Dr. **David Lane**, *University of Cambridge*
Dr. **Carol Leonard**, *University of Oxford*
Dr. **Maria Popova**, *McGill University, Montreal*

FOREIGN POLICY & INTERNATIONAL AFFAIRS
Dr. **Peter Duncan**, *University College London*
Prof. **Andreas Heinemann-Grüder**, *University of Bonn*
Prof. **Gerhard Mangott**, *University of Innsbruck*
Dr. **Diana Schmidt-Pfister**, *University of Konstanz*
Dr. **Lisbeth Tarlow**, *Harvard University, Cambridge*
Dr. **Christian Wipperfürth**, *N-Ost Network, Berlin*
Dr. **William Zimmerman**, *University of Michigan*

HISTORY, CULTURE & THOUGHT
Dr. **Catherine Andreyev**, *University of Oxford*
Prof. **Mark Bassin**, *Södertörn University*
Prof. **Karsten Brüggemann**, *Tallinn University*
Prof. **Alexander Etkind**, *Central European University*
Prof. **Gasan Gusejnov**, *Free University of Berlin*
Prof. **Leonid Luks**, *Catholic University of Eichstaett*
Dr. **Olga Malinova**, *Russian Academy of Sciences*
Dr. **Richard Mole**, *University College London*
Prof. **Andrei Rogatchevski**, *University of Tromsø*
Dr. **Mark Tauger**, *West Virginia University*

ADVISORY BOARD*

Prof. **Dominique Arel**, *University of Ottawa*
Prof. **Jörg Baberowski**, *Humboldt University of Berlin*
Prof. **Margarita Balmaceda**, *Seton Hall University*
Dr. **John Barber**, *University of Cambridge*
Prof. **Timm Beichelt**, *European University Viadrina*
Dr. **Katrin Boeckh**, *University of Munich*
Prof. em. **Archie Brown**, *University of Oxford*
Dr. **Vyacheslav Bryukhovetsky**, *Kyiv-Mohyla Academy*
Prof. **Timothy Colton**, *Harvard University, Cambridge*
Prof. **Paul D'Anieri**, *University of California*
Dr. **Heike Dörrenbächer**, *Friedrich Naumann Foundation*
Dr. **John Dunlop**, *Hoover Institution, Stanford, California*
Dr. **Sabine Fischer**, *SWP, Berlin*
Dr. **Geir Flikke**, *NUPI, Oslo*
Prof. **David Galbreath**, *University of Aberdeen*
Prof. **Frank Golczewski**, *University of Hamburg*
Dr. **Nikolas Gvosdev**, *Naval War College, Newport, RI*
Prof. **Mark von Hagen**, *Arizona State University*
Prof. **Guido Hausmann**, *University of Regensburg*
Prof. **Dale Herspring**, *Kansas State University*
Dr. **Stefani Hoffman**, *Hebrew University of Jerusalem*
Prof. em. **Andrzej Korbonski**, *University of California*
Dr. **Iris Kempe**, *"Caucasus Analytical Digest"*
Prof. **Herbert Küpper**, *Institut für Ostrecht Regensburg*
Prof. **Rainer Lindner**, *University of Konstanz*

Dr. **Luke March**, *University of Edinburgh*
Prof. **Michael McFaul**, *Stanford University, Palo Alto*
Prof. **Birgit Menzel**, *University of Mainz-Germersheim*
Dr. **Alex Pravda**, *University of Oxford*
Dr. **Erik van Ree**, *University of Amsterdam*
Dr. **Joachim Rogall**, *Robert Bosch Foundation Stuttgart*
Prof. **Peter Rutland**, *Wesleyan University, Middletown*
Prof. **Gwendolyn Sasse**, *University of Oxford*
Prof. **Jutta Scherrer**, *EHESS, Paris*
Prof. **Robert Service**, *University of Oxford*
Mr. **James Sherr**, *RIIA Chatham House London*
Dr. **Oxana Shevel**, *Tufts University, Medford*
Prof. **Eberhard Schneider**, *University of Siegen*
Prof. **Olexander Shnyrkov**, *Shevchenko University, Kyiv*
Prof. **Hans-Henning Schröder**, *SWP, Berlin*
Prof. **Yuri Shapoval**, *Ukrainian Academy of Sciences*
Dr. **Lisa Sundstrom**, *University of British Columbia*
Dr. **Philip Walters**, *"Religion, State and Society", Oxford*
Prof. **Zenon Wasyliw**, *Ithaca College, New York State*
Dr. **Lucan Way**, *University of Toronto*
Dr. **Markus Wehner**, *"Frankfurter Allgemeine Zeitung"*
Dr. **Andrew Wilson**, *University College London*
Prof. **Jan Zielonka**, *University of Oxford*
Prof. **Andrei Zorin**, *University of Oxford*

---

* While the Editorial Committee and Advisory Board support the General Editor in the choice and improvement of manuscripts for publication, responsibility for remaining errors and misinterpretations in the series' volumes lies with the books' authors.

Soviet and Post-Soviet Politics and Society (SPPS)
ISSN 1614-3515

Founded in 2004 and refereed since 2007, SPPS makes available affordable English-, German-, and Russian-language studies on the history of the countries of the former Soviet bloc from the late Tsarist period to today. It publishes between 5 and 20 volumes per year and focuses on issues in transitions to and from democracy such as economic crisis, identity formation, civil society development, and constitutional reform in CEE and the NIS. SPPS also aims to highlight so far understudied themes in East European studies such as right-wing radicalism, religious life, higher education, or human rights protection. The authors and titles of all previously published volumes are listed at the end of this book. For a full description of the series and reviews of its books, see www.ibidem-verlag.de/red/spps.

Editorial correspondence & manuscripts should be sent to: Dr. Andreas Umland, Department of Political Science, Kyiv-Mohyla Academy, vul. Voloska 8/5, UA-04070 Kyiv, UKRAINE; andreas.umland@cantab.net

Business correspondence & review copy requests should be sent to: *ibidem* Press, Leuschnerstr. 40, 30457 Hannover, Germany; tel.: +49 511 2622200; fax: +49 511 2622201; spps@ibidem.eu.

Authors, reviewers, referees, and editors for (as well as all other persons sympathetic to) SPPS are invited to join its networks at www.facebook.com/group.php?gid=52638198614
www.linkedin.com/groups?about=&gid=103012
www.xing.com/net/spps-ibidem-verlag/

Recent Volumes

272 Андреа Пето
Насилие и Молчание
Красная армия в Венгрии во Второй Мировой войн
ISBN 978-3-8382-1636-2

273 Winfried Schneider-Deters
Russia's War in Ukraine
Debates on Peace, Fascism, and War Crimes, 2022–2023
With a foreword by Klaus Gestwa
ISBN 978-3-8382-1876-2

274 Rasmus Nilsson
Uncanny Allies
Russia and Belarus on the Edge, 2012-2024
ISBN 978-3-8382-1288-3

275 Anton Grushetskyi, Volodymyr Paniotto
War and the Transformation of Ukrainian Society (2022–23)
Empirical Evidence
ISBN 978-3-8382-1944-8

276 Christian Kaunert, Alex MacKenzie, Adrien Nonjon (Eds.)
In the Eye of the Storm
Origins, Ideology, and Controversies of the Azov Brigade, 2014–23
ISBN 978-3-8382-1750-5

277 Gian Marco Moisé
The House Always Wins
The Corrupt Strategies that Shaped Kazakh Oil Politics and Business in the Nazarbayev Era
With a foreword by Alena Ledeneva
ISBN 978-3-8382-1917-2

278 Mikhail Minakov
The Post-Soviet Human
Philosophical Reflections on Social History after the End of Communism
ISBN 978-3-8382-1943-1

279 Natalia Kudriavtseva, Debra A. Friedman (eds.)
Language and Power in Ukraine and Kazakhstan
Essays on Education, Ideology, Literature, Practice, and the Media
With a foreword by Laada Bilaniuk
ISBN 978-3-8382-1949-3

280 Georges Mink, Iwona Reichardt (eds.)
The End of the Soviet World?
Essays on Post-Communist Political and Social Change
With an afterword by Richardt Butterwick
ISBN 978-3-8382-1961-5

Contents

Introduction. Teaching IR in Wartime. Pedagogical Adaptations and Theoretical Challenges
Kateryna Zarembo and Michèle Knodt 7

Teaching the Russian War Against Ukraine. Ukraine as a Microcosm of the Paradigm Shift from International Relations to Planetary Politics
Ian Manners 21

Eastern Europe Marginalized in Teaching IR. Lessons Learned from Russia's War Against Ukraine
Olena Khylko 53

Teaching International Political Economy in Times of War
Thomas Fetzer 85

From Shock to Adaptation Through National Unity and Action. Third-Year Undergraduate Students of First Eighty Days of Russia's War Against Ukraine
Galyna Solovei 103

An Essay from a Rector. The Challenges and Rewards of Teaching During Wartime
Tymofii Brik 123

About the Authors (in Alphabetical Order) 135
About the Editors 137

Introduction
Teaching IR in Wartime
Pedagogical Adaptations and Theoretical Challenges

Kateryna Zarembo and Michèle Knodt

The ongoing Russian war against Ukraine has brought many new challenges to the teaching of IR.[1] While scholars around the world have been engaged in multiple debates over the "correct" theories, explanatory fit, policy prescriptions and predictions of the outcome of the largest interstate war in Europe since the end of World War II, Ukrainian scholars have struggled to deliver lectures from the bomb shelters, under occupation, or from the front lines.

Observing and participating in these debates, we have chosen to focus in this volume on the question of how this war has changed our approach not only to thinking about but also to teaching IR. As educators, we are in a position to have a direct impact on the minds of the next generations of citizens around the world — so what lessons have we learned, and how has our teaching of IR changed in response to the unlawful and hitherto unpunished territorial aggression and massive war crimes in the heart of Europe? We have therefore published a call for papers, inviting the academic community to reflect on the following questions: What new challenges have emerged in teaching IR in the context of the Russian war against Ukraine? How have lecturers incorporated the war into their IR courses, and what impact has it had on the content and focus of the courses? How have university lecturers adapted their teaching methods to remote and hybrid learning environments?

---

1   While the war has been ongoing since 2014, this volume was inspired by the new wave of discussions on the utility of IR theories and revision thereof as well as the changes in teaching and learning conditions in Ukraine in the aftermath of the Russian full-scale invasion in Ukraine in 2022.

What role has technology and digital tools played in facilitating IR education during the war? How have lecturers addressed the emotional and psychological impact of the war on students, and how have they supported their wellbeing?

The contributions selected as the result of this call and appearing in the present volume tackle these questions from a variety of perspectives. Before we present them, let us briefly outline the literature landscape to which this volume contributes. We have identified two major trends in the available literature. One is a rather copious corpus of texts that depict the Russian war against Ukraine as a stimulus for theory confirmation or development — that is, either reaffirming that an existing theory (predominantly realism) has proved useful and functional or challenging it in an overwhelmingly postcolonial vein. The other, mainly represented by Ukrainian voices, describes the teaching realia of the Ukrainian educators during the full-scale invasion: admittedly, this trend is not constrained to teaching IR but is rather related to the state of education and educators under attack regardless of the discipline.

Before we briefly familiarize the reader with both trends, a caveat should be placed. While this volume focuses on the experiences connected to Ukraine, we do not mean to limit the topic of teaching IR in wartime to Ukrainian experience or context. While we do believe that the Russian war against Ukraine leads to the reset of the post-WWII world order, we are also aware of the fact that, as of 2024, the populations of 42 countries are affected by various types of violence[2] according to the World Population Review, with their impact reaching far beyond the national borders. Hence, we rely on the case we know best (and, in the case of some editors and authors, have a direct relation to) in order to arrive at the conclusions and practices applicable to other contexts.

---

2   https://worldpopulationreview.com/country-rankings/countries-currently-at-war

Russian war against Ukraine: a turning point in IR theory or not?

From a theoretical perspective, the Russian invasion of Ukraine has provoked a massive debate within IR theory. Costa and Blanc (2024) even argue that a "full-fledged inter-state war, and the possibility of a great-power war, returns IR to its post-World War I roots" (p. 24), breathing new life into the grand theoretical debate, which was "reduced to a handy hermeneutic tool, apt only for teaching purposes when first exposing undergraduate students to IR theory" (p.23). In theoretical debates, the Russian invasion has provoked both the renaissance of mainstream IR theories, especially realism, and, at the same time, their vocal contestation.

Thus, according to Pietrzak (2024), "[in]sensitive as it sounds, Russia's war in Ukraine may be the best thing that has happened to the realist IR theory for quite some time" (p. 11). In a similar vein, Stephen Walt (2022) also claims that one could hardly look for a more convincing demonstration of the relevance of hard, especially military, power, although he carefully underlines that explanation does not equal justification.

However, the critical approach to the realist premises has been no less vocal. The open-access journal *Analyse & Kritik*, published by De Gruyter, devoted an issue in November 2022 to a reappraisal of realism inspired by the Russian invasion. The editorial states that "Mearsheimer's analysis, which appears at first sight to be strikingly fitting to the brutal act, becomes less convincing upon closer inspection," referring to the American realist John Mearsheimer's long-standing explanation of the Russian actions that overlooks Ukraine's agency. Contributors to the issue point to the mistakes of the realists, such as an over-reliance on rationalism, when leaders who start wars rarely behave rationally (Lebow 2022).

Others are even more categorical: "Among the collateral damage of the war in Ukraine is a school of thought: realism" (Poast 2022). This point is developed further by Dutkiewicz and Smolenski (2023), who argue that the realist approach to explaining

Russia's war against Ukraine is a perfect example of what they call "epistemic superimposition," in which abstract theories are superimposed on unique historical and political contexts up to the point of anti-empiricism, with facts selected to fit the presumption of the theory. The authors reiterate the point made earlier by Maria Mälksoo that "the difficulties of arguably most important IR theory to properly understand and appreciate the resistance of Ukrainians to Russian aggression tells us a lot about the colonial predicament of IR as a discipline" (Dutkiewicz and Smolenski 2023, 627).

This point has been taken up by other critical scholars, leading to a wave of research and publications on decolonization and knowledge production in social sciences in general and in IR specifically in particular (among the most prominent examples of the debate are Hendl, Burlyuk, O'Sullivan and Arystanbek as well as the special issue edited by Burlyuk and Musliu 2023 under the provocative title "Responsibility to remain silent"). Terms such as "epistemic imperialism" (Sonevytsky 2022) and "epistemic injustice" has been coined to denote the hierarchy of knowledge production, where someone's knowledge (defined by positionality, i.e., the country of origin, the availability of resources, etc) and right to produce knowledge is considered more legitimate than others. This is firmly tied to the imperial or colonial background of the respective academic environments. As Moore (2001), cited by Pishchikova, rightly argues, defining some (e.g., Russo-Soviet) colonialism as a deviation while holding the other (e.g., Franco-British) as a universal standard is a form of epistemic coloniality in itself. Pishchikova further observes: "Just as feminist writers lamented being dismissed because they made knowledge claims that seemed too personal and too emotional to be 'credible' and 'authoritative,' scholars *of* and *from* Ukraine make a plea for the acceptance of their particular state of trauma, grief, and rage as a legitimate position for knowledge production (Pishchikova 2023, 102)". Thus, in the field of IR, as in many others in social sciences and beyond, the Russian war spurred yet another debate about who is entitled to talk and to be listened to, as well as how to listen, research and respond to the challenges of the war zone (Sereda, Mikheieva 2025).

Teaching about the war while living through it: challenges of (non)-embodied knowledge

Some empathetic IR scholars, such as Toros et al. (2018), have already questioned the dilemma that has been roughly sketched above: how "to bridge the gap between war theorizing, occurring in universities mostly in the West, and war experience, mostly occurring elsewhere?" Sylvester (2012, 492, quoted in Toros) observed that IR research "place[s] the researcher at some physical and psychic distance" from the object of study, at least in its "traditional" way of conduct. However, this does not apply anymore since some researchers both live through the war and teach war at the same time. Importantly, "some of us live war because of *who* we are and not *where* we are" (Toros et al. 2018) — this point is echoed by many Ukrainian scholars who experienced the war from abroad or involuntarily became refugees.

A number of papers have been published on the impact of the war on Ukrainian educators, students and academia (e.g., Kurapov et al. 2024, Lavrysh et al. 2022, Tsybuliak et al. 2024). According to the World Bank, "one in five of Ukraine's higher education institutions have been damaged or destroyed during the ongoing Russian invasion. For research institutions, the rate rises to 31%." However, the calculations may be imprecise because it is impossible to estimate the destruction in the temporarily occupied territories fully. As of January 2024, 13.5% of the academic staff in Ukraine have been internally displaced or become refugees abroad (UNESCO 2024). Overall, the full-scale war has affected the Ukrainian higher education sphere by the following factors, summarized by Antoniuk (2022, 8):

> "1) large-scale destruction of higher education facilities [...]; 2) a direct threat to the life and health of students and academic staff; 3) the necessity

of forced relocation of higher educational institutions from the zone of hostilities [...]; 4) the loss of educational and production practice bases for students as a result of the destruction or relocation of enterprises; 5) a significant loss of the contingent of students and pedagogical and teaching staff as a result of migration and [conscription]; 6) use of educational facilities for other purposes; 7) decrease in financial resources of higher education institutions; and 8) the loss of managerial educational control over higher education institutions in the territories that have come under temporary occupation or are in the zone of active [hostilities]."

Zooming in on specific cases, some published papers offer solution-oriented approaches and best practices for dealing with the changed circumstances. One of the most notable examples is the "University without Walls" (Lopatina et al. 2023), which has become a reality for the Berdyansk State Pedagogical University. As the city of Berdyansk has remained temporarily occupied since 2022, the university had to relocate to Zaporizhzhia but still could not work on the ground due to security conditions (the city of Zaporizhzhia is at the frontline and within the range of artillery shelling at the time of writing). Hence, the university community shifted to working as an online asynchronous mode ("where university staff and students can be separated by time and space yet still communicate effectively"), while its members were physically placed all over, from occupied Berdyansk to the state-controlled territory of Ukraine to abroad. This studying format was called the "University without Walls" after the 1971 University of Massachusetts experiment.

Another important example of academic resilience is the Invisible University for Ukraine, launched by the Central European University for undergraduate and postgraduate students from Ukraine, regardless of their place of residence. As the program webpage explains, "the name of this transnational solidarity program evokes the various nineteenth and twentieth-century underground and exile educational initiatives (such as the "flying universities") in Eastern Europe, as well as the tradition of Invisible Colleges formed after 1989 in the region."[3]

---

3   https://www.ceu.edu/non-degree/Invisible-University

Even less has been written about how the war has affected the teaching of specific disciplines. An important exception is an article by Amy Kenworthy and Sophia Opatska (Kenworthy, Opatska 2023), in which the latter, the founding dean of the business school and vice-rector for strategic development of the Ukrainian Catholic University in Lviv, presented the technique of adapting the classroom work at the start of the invasion. At the core of service-learning is the idea of applying the theory the students learn in the classroom to real-world problems and needs. So, in their class of international business, the class activities were adapted so that "every aspect of what [they] did related to how [they] could affect positive change in business and organizational environments to support Ukraine, and Ukrainian people, through [their] work." (Kenworthy and Opatska 2023, 422).

However, there has been little reflection on how the war affected the teaching of specific disciplines, namely IR. It is precisely this gap that this volume seeks to fill.

Mapping changes in teaching IR in theoretical approaches and everyday practices

This volume brings together a diverse team of contributors who offer their views from various disciplines (IR, international political economy, conflict studies, diplomacy studies, European studies and philosophy), professional backgrounds, places of residence, engagement with the war and national origins. Three out of the six authors are Ukrainian by citizenship. One author resided in Ukraine at the time of writing their contribution, and two others experienced forced migration abroad as a result of the invasion in 2022. The contributors also come from and represent a variety of theoretical schools and empirical approaches, as presented in their chapters.

Ian Manners, Olena Khylko and Thomas Fetzer explore the consequences of the Russian War against Ukraine for teaching IR theory, offering a panoramic view of the tendencies and changes or lack thereof.

In his contribution, Ian Manners draws on longitudinal research publication trends generated using the Clarivate Web of Science Social Science Citation Index (SSCI) as well as on his experience of teaching IR and European Union (EU) studies at eight universities in four different countries from 1991 to 2024. He argues that the neoimperial perspective on Ukraine and the neglect of its existence, let alone stakes, in teaching IR and EU studies in the last three decades is another instance of academic shortsightedness and belongs together with the neglect of environmental unsustainability. Manners also observes a worrying trend that even in the updated IR textbooks, the Russian invasion is perceived as a case for conventional IR theory rather than a wake-up call to rethink the global world order. He concludes with five recommendations for "shifting IR teaching away from 19th-century geopolitics and four-power multipolarism, and towards 21st-century planetary politics that escapes the binary paradigm of the past 75 years" (Manners 2025, this volume).

Olena Khylko's chapter engages in a dialogue with Manner's chapter by examining any changes that have taken place so far since 2022 in the teaching curricula. Having analyzed pre- and post-2022 syllabi on IR theory and postcolonial studies from 27 North American and European universities, she concluded that Russia's war against Ukraine brought about few to no changes in the teaching of IR studies in Western academic institutions. Not only is it indicative of the "unreadiness of Western academia to question the explanatory value of the mainstream IR theories" (Khykko 2025, this volume), but it also signals the double marginalization of Eastern European postcolonial experiences and cases in contrast to the broader inclusiveness of the Global South scholarship, at the detriment to the principle of integrative pluralism and "pluriversity" in IR for which Khylko advocates.

The article by Thomas Fetzer addresses the challenges of teaching international political economy (IPE) in the context of the

Russo-Ukrainian war in view of the discipline's historical neglect of war and security issues evident in textbooks and leading journals. The article then proposes two pedagogical approaches to address this gap. First, it advocates for a critical engagement with mainstream IPE approaches, highlighting their shortcomings in explaining the Russian war against Ukraine. The author suggests using the war to illustrate how liberal and neo-Marxist IPE paradigms shape perceptions of the economy-security nexus. Second, the article explores the concept of "weaponized interdependence" as a crucial tool for analyzing the war's impact on IR. This concept challenges traditional assumptions of economic interdependence leading to peace and cooperation. Instead, it emphasizes how states can strategically exploit economic ties for geopolitical gain, as illustrated by Russia's use of energy resources. The piece concludes by emphasizing the need for critical reflection on the normative dimensions and political implications involved in teaching IPE during wartime.

In their turn, Galyna Solovei and Tymofiy Brik provide insights into teaching challenges and insights on the ground as warzone academics.

Galyna Solovei's chapter offers a unique glimpse into the teaching realia of the first months of the war. When the invasion caught her teaching the "Introduction to the Peace and Conflict Studies" to third-year students, she realized that she had to adapt her teaching to meet the students' needs amid the earthquake-like changes around. Relying on Judith Herman's framework she asked students to self-assess their psychological state and coherently describe their experiences of three months of war. In her chapter, she presents the analysis of these essays, giving a voice to Ukrainian students as the bearers of firsthand embodied knowledge of what war is like. She identifies three overarching themes and reflects on the classroom work as a resilience-building exercise for students. Solovei's chapter makes a priceless contribution to the volume as an example of adaptive teaching techniques in changing circumstances and, at the same time, a discourse analysis paper built on unique ethnographic material, timely collected and preserved.

Finally, the contribution by Tymofiy Brik reflects on the challenges and rewards of teaching during wartime, specifically focusing on the experiences of Ukrainian educators during the Russian invasion. The author, a researcher and rector at the Kyiv School of Economics (KSE), highlights the resilience of the Ukrainian academic space, showcased by the adaptability of universities, which became community hubs and centers of research and defense innovation. The KSE, for instance, adapted by providing online courses, constructing bomb shelters, and launching new programs addressing urgent societal needs, attracting a significant increase in enrollment. The author emphasizes the crucial role of IR, both as a discipline and as a daily practice, in navigating the crisis, highlighting the need for active engagement in global diplomacy. The author concludes that universities are not merely centers of learning but agents of change, vital for fostering resilience and rebuilding a nation. The experiences described offer valuable lessons for universities facing similar challenges globally.

Conclusions

This volume offers a multifaceted exploration of teaching IR during the ongoing Russian war against Ukraine. Contributors, including Ukrainian and international academics, share diverse perspectives on the challenges and adaptations necessitated by changing global circumstances. The chapters reveal a shift in IR pedagogy, moving beyond theoretical debates to address the immediate realities of war. The experiences highlight the limitations of traditional IR theories in fully grasping the complexities of the war and underscore the importance of incorporating lived experiences and diverse voices into the classroom.

Contributors emphasize the need for greater reflexivity in IR teaching, acknowledging the political and ethical implications of knowledge production in wartime. The volume demonstrates the resilience of Ukrainian academia, its adaptability in the face of adversity, and the crucial role of international collaboration in sustaining educational efforts. Ultimately, this collection serves as a valuable resource for educators seeking to integrate the lessons of the war into IR curricula, promoting a more nuanced, context-aware, and critically engaged approach to the field. The insights provided extend beyond the specific context of Russia's war against Ukraine, offering valuable lessons for resilience and global understanding facilitated by revising the established paradigms and approaches.

References

Antoniuk, Valentyna. 2023. "Perspective Chapter: The War as a Factor of Upheavals and Transformations in Higher Education – Experience of Ukraine." In *Higher Education – Reflections from the Field – Volume 1*, edited by Edward Everett, 1–26. London: IntechOpen. DOI: http://dx.doi.org/10.5772/intechopen.109688.

Burlyuk, Olga, and Viosa Musliu, eds. 2023. "The Responsibility to Remain Silent? On the Politics of Knowledge Production, Expertise and (Self-)Reflection in Russia's War Against Ukraine." *Journal of International Relations and Development*, 26(4).

Costa, Oriel, Martínez Blanc, C. 2024. Back to the Roots? The War in Ukraine and Grand Theories in International Relations. In: Wiesner, C., Knodt, M. (eds) *The War Against Ukraine and the EU*. Palgrave Macmillan, Cham. https://doi.org/10.1007/978-3-031-35040-5_2

Dutkiewicz, J., and J. Smolenski. 2023. "Epistemic Superimposition: The War in Ukraine and the Poverty of Expertise in International Relations Theory." *Journal of International Relations and Development*, 26: 619–31.

Hendl, Tereza, Olga Burlyuk, Mila O'Sullivan, and Aizada Arystanbek. 2023. "(En)Countering Epistemic Imperialism: A Critique of 'Westsplaining' and Coloniality in Dominant Debates on Russia's Invasion of Ukraine." *Contemporary Security Policy* 45 (2): 171–209. doi: 10.1080/13523260.2023.2288468.

Kenworthy, Amy L., and Sophia Opatska. 2023. "Teaching During War in Ukraine: Service-Learning as a Tool for Facilitating Student Learning and Engagement During Times of Uncertainty and Crisis." *Journal of Management Education*, 47(4): 417–39. DOI: 10.1177/10525629231166695.

Kurapov Anton, Valentyna Pavlenko, Alexander Drozdov, Nataliia Korchakova & Iuliia Pavlova. 2024. Impact of War on Ukrainian University Students and Personnel: Repeated Cross-Sectional Study, *Journal of Loss and Trauma* DOI: 10.1080/15325024.2024.2433990

Lavrysh, Yuliana, Iryna Lytovchenko, Valentyna Lukianenko, and Tetiana Golub. 2022. "Teaching during the Wartime: Experience from Ukraine." *Educational Philosophy and Theory*, July, 1–8. doi: 10.1080/00131857.2022.2098714.

Lopatina, Hanna, Natalia Tsybuliak, Anastasia Popova, Ihor Bohdanov and Yana Suchikova (2023). University without Walls: Experience of Berdyansk State Pedagogical University during the war. *Problems and Perspectives in Management*, 21(2-si), 4-14. doi: 10.21511/ppm.21(2-si).2023.02

Mälksoo, Maria. 2022. "The Postcolonial Moment in Russia's War Against Ukraine." *Journal of Genocide Research* 25 (3–4): 471–81. doi:10.1080/14623528.2022.2074947.

Moore, D. C. 2001. "Is the Post- in Postcolonial the Post- in Post-Soviet? Toward a Global Postcolonial Critique." *PMLA*, 116 (1): 111–28.

Lebow, Richard Ned. 2022. "International Relations Theory and the Ukrainian War." *Analyse & Kritik*, 44(1): 111–35. https://doi.org/10.1515/auk-2022-2021.

Pietrzak, Piotr. 2024. "The Russia–Ukraine War and the Renaissance of IR Realism." *Forum Nauk Społecznych*, 2 (2024): 9–23. doi:10.31648/fns.10108.

Pishchikova, Kateryna. 2023. "What Ukraine Teaches Us About International Relations and Vice Versa." *IdPS Interdisciplinary Political Studies*, 9(2): 97-107. https://doi.org/10.1285/i20398573v9n2p97

Sereda, Viktoriya, and Oksana Mikheieva. 2025. "How (Not) to Study a War-Affected Society: Challenges of Knowledge Production in Ukraine and Elsewhere." *Nationalities Papers*, 1–20. https://doi.org/10.1017/nps.2024.56.

Sonevytsky, Maria. 2022. "What is Ukraine? Notes on epistemic imperialism". *Topos*, no. 2 (December), 21-30. https://doi.org/10.24412/1815-0047-2022-2-21-30.

Sylvester, Christine. 2012. "War Experiences/War Practices/War Theory." *Millennium: Journal of International Studies* 40: 483-503.

Toros, Harmonie, Daniel Dunleavy, Joe Gazeley, Alex Guirakhoo, Lucie Merian, and Yasmeen Omran. 2018. "Where is War? We Are War." Teaching and Learning the Human Experience of War in the Classroom. *International Studies Perspectives*, 19 (3), 199-217.

Tsybuliak, Natalia, Hanna Lopatina, Liudmyla Shevchenko, et al. 2024. "Researchers of Ukrainian Universities in Wartime Conditions: Needs, Challenges and Opportunities." *Regional Science Policy & Practice*, 16 (9), https://doi.org/10.1016/j.rspp.2024.100012.

UNESCO. 2024. *Analysis of War Damage to the Ukrainian Science Sector and its Consequences*. Paris: UNESCO. ISBN 978-92-3-100662-3.

Walt, Stephen M. 2022. "An International Relations Theory Guide to the War in Ukraine." *Foreign Policy*, March 8.

Teaching the Russian War Against Ukraine
Ukraine as a Microcosm of the Paradigm Shift from International Relations to Planetary Politics

Ian Manners[1]

The 30-year period of Ukrainian independence after the collapse of the Soviet Union did not feature much, if at all, in the teaching of IR in western European universities. The 2013–2014 Maidan Revolution and 2014 Russian annexation of Crimea and the Donbas featured as interesting events in IR, while the 2016 EU-Ukraine Free Trade Area and 2017 Association Agreement were also interesting to EU studies. However, neither Ukraine nor these events were widely taught in western European IR or EU studies prior to the Russian invasion on 24 February 2022. This article analyzes the impact of the Russian war against Ukraine on the teaching of IR and EU studies in Europe. It argues that Ukrainian resistance to the invasion is part of an important shift in thinking about IR and the EU in empirical and theoretical terms, as well as accelerating a changed pedagogic paradigm to teaching IR and EU studies within holistic planetary politics.

    The article does this in four steps by drawing on personal experiences of teaching, research publications and textbooks from the period 1991–2024. First, the article introduces the terminologies and technologies of teaching IR and EU studies, Ukraine and Russia, EU enlargement and the "post-Soviet space" after the end of the Cold War. Second, the article analyzes the conventional teaching of IR and EU studies in Western Europe, 1991–2022, by looking at what

---

1   I am very grateful to Kateryna Zarembo, Michèle Knodt, Maksym Yakovlyev, Thomas Fetzer, Mridula Ghosh, Olena Khylko, Galyna Solovei, Nina Krickel-Choi, Simon Stattin, Ted Svensson, and Anders Uhlin for their thoughtful reflections and critical comments.

was included and excluded in the study of these disciplines using Clarivate Web of Science (SSCI). Third, the article examines the transformation of teaching IR and EU studies after the invasion and counter-offensive of 2022–2024, focusing on the rapid process of re-education and rethinking of teaching about Ukraine and Russia in IR and EU studies courses. Fourth, the article concludes by thinking ahead to the necessary paradigm shift to teaching planetary politics that the Russian war against Ukraine and other 21st-century crises demand. This paradigm shift centers the planet as a whole and de-centers Western and Eurocentric IR and EU studies, ensuring that peripheralized, marginalized, or colonized subjects such as post-colonial Africa, Asia, or post-Soviet Eastern Europe, as well as ecology, stateless peoples, and planetary justice, are properly part of constituting 21st century planetary politics. Thus, the article argues the need to understand Ukraine as a microcosm of symbiotic planetary politics, an example of the wider planetary organic crisis of five symbiotic dimensions of economy, society, ecology, conflict, and polity.

My personal experiences of teaching, research publication, and textbooks come from teaching IR and EU studies at the University of Bristol, Swansea University, University of Kent, Brussels School of International Studies, Malmö University, Roskilde University, University of Copenhagen, and Lund University from 1991 to 2024. During this period, the author taught IR and EU studies at both undergraduate and postgraduate levels almost every year for three decades and has seen trends and fashions come and go. Nevertheless, during this period, these two disciplines have become more confident about teaching disciplinary history and theory as the core, much to the expense of peripheral, marginal, or colonized subjects such as Ukraine. This article addresses this problem by asking questions about the new teaching challenges driven by the Russian invasion of Ukraine.

1. Introduction: Teaching the Russian War Against Ukraine

> Americans and Europeans were guided through the new century by a tale about "the end of history," by what I will call the *politics of inevitability*, a sense that the future is just more of the present, that the laws of progress are known, that there are not alternatives, and therefore nothing really to be done.... Americans and Europeans kept telling themselves their tales of inevitability for a quarter of a century after the end of communism, and so raised a millennial generation without history.... The fates of Russia, Ukraine, and Belarus after 1991 showed well enough that the fall of one system did not create a blank slate on which nature generated markets and markets generated rights (Snyder 2018: 7).

The terminologies and technologies of teaching IR and EU studies in western European universities evolved rapidly with the end of the Cold War and the birth of the "New Europe" following Timothy Snyder's "politics of inevitability." Narrating the interim period 1991–2022 in terms of teaching IR is impossible; every teaching experience was and is so different, Europe West and Europe East, Global North and Global South. However, there are two features that Timothy Snyder, one of the leading scholars of IR in and between Russia, Europe, and America, uses to describe this period: the *politics of inevitability* and the *politics of eternity*. The *politics of inevitability* since the 1980s is the assumption that there is no alternative to neoliberalism, defined as the privatization of public life, including the deregulation and privatization of nationalized industries, financial services, the welfare state, and government (Manners 2018, 1225). While these neoliberal assumptions survived the global financial crisis (GFC) of 2007–2008 and the Eurozone sovereign debt crisis of 2009–2012, the COVID-19 pandemic and the return of the *politics of eternity* challenged hyper-globalization. In contrast, the *politics of eternity* "places one nation at the center of a cyclical story of victimhood" where "eternity politicians manufacture crisis and manipulate the resultant emotion" (Snyder 2018, 8). The past 18 years of democratic decline since 2005 have seen the rise of the *politics of eternity* and eternity politicians across the world (Freedom House 2024).

Reflecting personally on teaching based on syllabi and textbooks provides one route to the experiences of teaching IR and EU studies prior to and after the Russian invasion of Ukraine. Having taught courses in IR and EU studies in seven different departments across at least three different countries brings some comparative experience and overview of teaching. These personal reflections will be strengthened by using and developing Felix Berenskötter's (2018) review of "How textbooks cover theories" to assess what extent and how transatlantic IR textbooks cover theories and issues in contemporary IR. A second route to understanding the changes in teaching IR in wartime is to examine the intellectual context in which teaching takes place through a series of longitudinal research publication trends generated using the Clarivate Web of Science SSCI. While SSCI generates a number of analytical problems, it does help provide an overview of the incidence of certain research terms in IR during 1990-2023.[2] In Section 2, the research terms include "Ukraine," "Crimea," "Donbas(s)" and "environmental," "climate change," and "green." In Section 3, the research terms include "geopolitics," "multipolar," and "neoimperial/neocolonial." In the concluding Section 4, the research terms include "ecology," "climate crisis/emergency," and "planetary politics." These analyses show how the core of IR and EU studies focus on certain subjects, such as geopolitics, in contrast to the peripheralized Ukraine and the climate crisis. Where possible, these terms will also be used to examine the textbooks.

The article then provides both a personal experience of an international university professor during the Russian war against Ukraine but also tries to narrate the terminologies and technologies of teaching IR and EU studies. The analysis of syllabi and textbooks illustrates the changing technologies of teaching IR and EU studies. The analysis of both (pre-)wartime terms and planetary political terms illustrates the changing terminologies of teaching IR and EU

---

2   The SSCI produces path-dependent citation patterns emphasising US-institutional bias.

studies. The combination of these analyses leads to the argument that Ukrainian resistance to the Russian invasion is part of an important shift in thinking about IR and the EU in empirical and theoretical terms, accelerating the need for a change in pedagogic paradigms to teaching IR and EU studies.

2. International Relations of the 20th Century

> *The General Assembly,*
> *Reaffirming* the paramount importance of the Charter of the United Nations in the promotion of the rule of law among nations,
> 1. *Affirms* its commitment to the sovereignty, political independence, unity and territorial integrity of Ukraine within its internationally recognized borders;
> 2. *Calls upon* all States to desist and refrain from actions aimed at the partial or total disruption of the national unity and territorial integrity of Ukraine, including any attempts to modify Ukraine's borders through the threat or use of force or other unlawful means;
> (United Nations (UN) General Assembly Resolution 68/262 2014)

In general, the teaching of IR over the past 100 years has focused on the conservative state-centric concerns of the 20th century, placing the League of Nations and the UN at the center of study. The February to March 2014 Russian occupation and annexation of Ukrainian Crimea and Donbas led to the 7th March 2014 UN GA resolution 68/262 on the "Territorial integrity of Ukraine" (above). One hundred members voted to defend the principles of the UN Charter and international peace. Ninety-three members declined to defend the UN and international peace. While the failure of so many members to defend UN principles was not unique, this vote and subsequent UN GA votes in 2022 marked the end of 20th-century IR.

Early post-Cold War courses and textbooks were marked by a simultaneous loosening of the intellectual straitjacket and the desire to repack the period into existing intellectual frames. The earliest IR textbooks to capture the post-Cold War shift in thinking included Burchill and Linklater (1996), Brown (1997), and Baylis and Smith (1997). In contrast, the earliest EU textbooks included Nugent

(1994), Wallace and Wallace (1996), McCormick (1999), and Bretherton and Vogler (1999). None of these textbooks considered Ukraine to any extent except as a brief historical footnote in the dissolution of the Soviet Union. Instead, IR and EU courses mixed the 'classical' story of IR state-centrism with the 'new' story of IR borderless liberalism. The neoliberal aspects of IR, such as globalization and corporatization, focused on the "globalization of world politics" (Baylis, Smith, and Owens 2022) and "supraterritoriality" (Scholte 2000), which left Ukraine and its sovereignty, democracy, and politics to the markets of the *politics of inevitability*. The neostatist aspects of IR, such as nationalism and egoism, focused on "how states think" (Mearsheimer and Rosato 2023) and "rationality in foreign policy" (Stein 2016), which left Ukraine and its sovereignty, security, and politics to the power games of the *politics of eternity*.

During 2000–2004, I taught a master's course, "European Union Enlargement," which included topics on Belarus, Moldova, Ukraine, Armenia, Azerbaijan, and Georgia (Manners 1999, 2010). However, in general, during this period, there were a number of aspects of Ukraine that we did not teach, such as the 1000-year-old origins of European Kyivan Rus or Ukraine as a founding member of the UN in 1945, and there were a number that we mistaught such as the acquiescence of Ukraine in the Soviet Union and the idea of post-Cold War Eastern Europe as a "post-soviet space." As charts 1 and 2 (below) demonstrate, IR research on Ukraine, Crimea, and Donbas broadly reflected this absence of teaching and textbook consideration during the period 1990–2014, but also the belated inclusion of these topics since the Russian occupation and invasion of Ukraine.

Charts 1 and 2: SSCI references to "International Relations," "Ukraine," "Crimea," and "Donbas(s)," 1990–2023 expressed absolutely and in percentages.

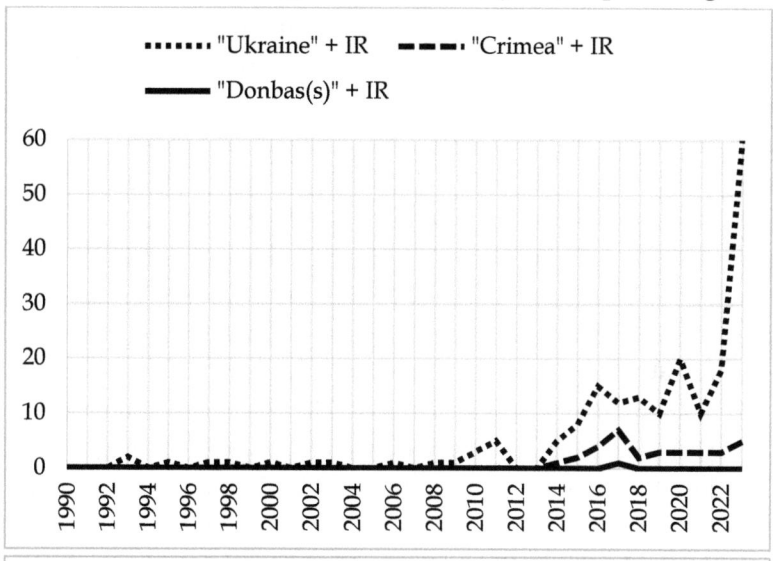

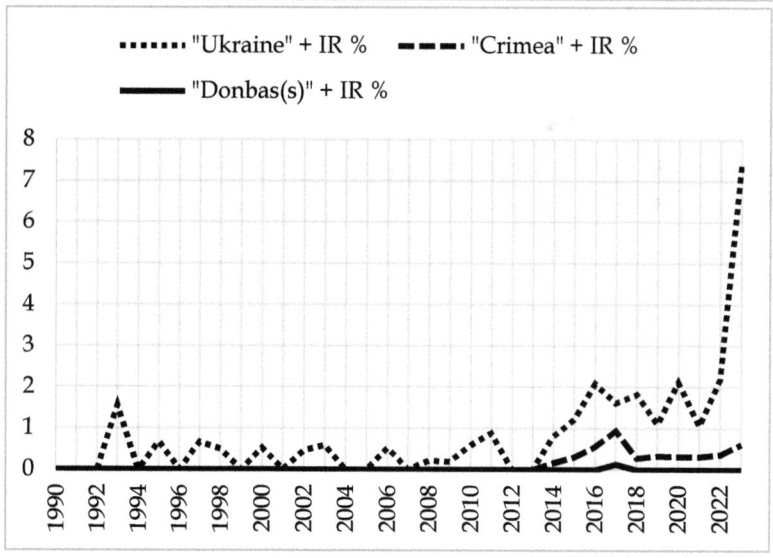

Chart 1 (left) shows the comparative incidence of the phrases "International Relations" plus "Ukraine," "Crimea," and "Donbas(s)" from 1990 to 2023 in the SSCI. A few references to Ukraine occurred during the 1990s and have increased steadily since the 2014 Russian occupation of Crimea and Donbas. Articles referring to Crimea increased after 2014, but Donbas references are effectively zero. Chart 2 (right) shows the comparative incidence of the phrases "International Relations" plus "Ukraine," "Crimea," and "Donbas(s)" as a percentage of the incidence of the phrase "International Relations" from 1990 to 2023 in the SSCI. This chart makes it possible to see whether references to Ukraine, Crimea, and Donbas are more or less common as a proportion of published articles over time. The chart shows that there was an interest in research articles between 1991 Ukrainian independence, 2004–2005 Orange Revolution, and 2013–2014 Maidan Revolution at less than 1% of overall IR articles. The 2014 Russian occupation and the 2022 Russian invasion led to a growth of over 7% of IR articles in 2023. Articles referring to "Crimea" peaked in 2017 (1% of IR articles), and "Donbas(s)" peaked in 2020 following the Russian occupation of these Ukrainian regions.

Overall, the IR research community had very little interest in Ukraine, Crimea, and Donbas in the 25 years from 1990 to 2014. However, Ukraine is hardly unique in this respect. To think more holistically about blind spots in IR teaching and research, the article will compare Ukraine with the broad issue of environmental climate change. Russia's status as both a "petrostate" and one of the world's worst fossil fuel polluters enables it to invade Ukraine and use "ecocide" as a weapon; hence, the comparison facilitates the discussion of planetary politics. Similar to charts 1 and 2, charts 3 and 4 (below) compare the absolute and relative references to "environmental," "climate change," and "green" in IR research.

Charts 3 and 4: SSCI references to "International Relations," "Green," "Environmental," and "Climate Change" 1990–2023 expressed absolutely and in percentages

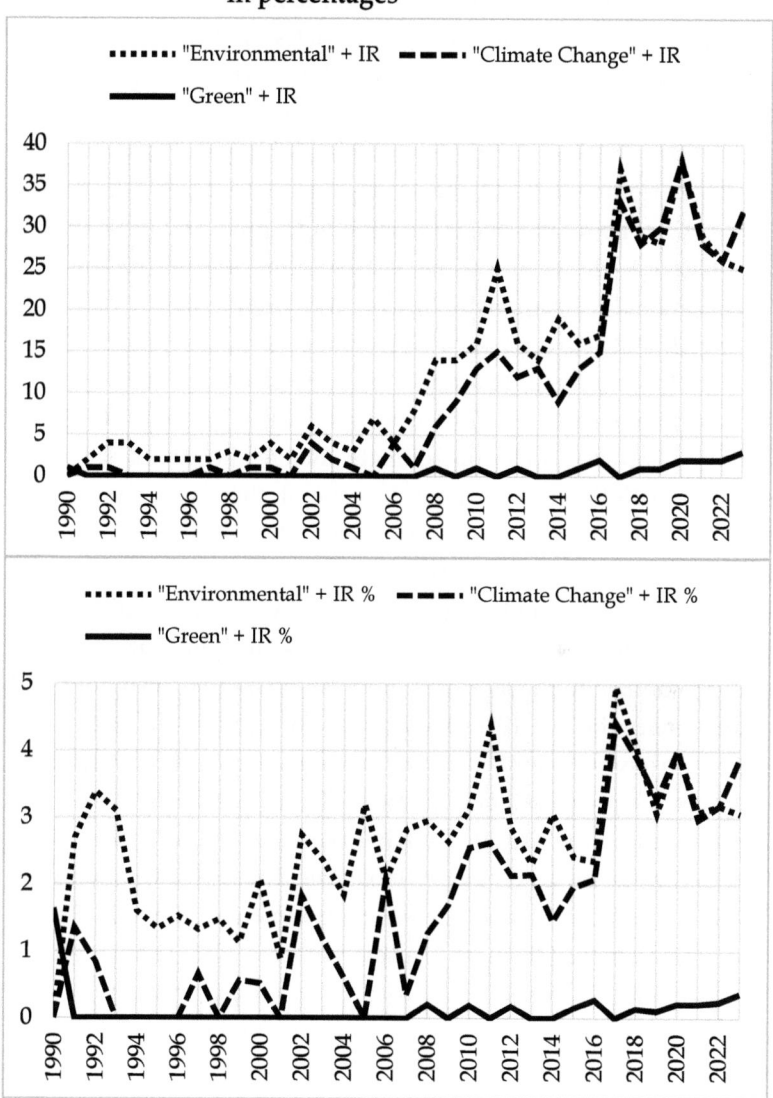

Chart 3 (left) shows the relative occurrence of the phrases "International Relations" plus "Environmental," "Climate Change," and "Green" in SSCI articles from 1990 to 2023. Articles on "environmental" IR increased steadily from 1991 to 2011 and surged in 2017 and 2020 before declining in 2023. Articles on "Climate Change" and IR grew slowly between 2007 and 2017. Articles surged in 2020 before declining in 2022. Articles on "Green" IR have emerged slowly over the past decade but are not significant. The average of 25–40 environmental and climate change articles per year during 2017–2023 is about half the 60 articles on Ukraine and IR in 2023.

Chart 4 (right) shows the relative occurrence of the phrases "International Relations" plus "Environmental," "Climate Change," and "Green" as a percentage of the incidence of the phrase "International Relations" in the SSCI 1990 to 2023. Articles on "environmental" IR were erratically higher in 1992, 2011, and 2017. In contrast, articles on "climate change" increased above 3% after the 2015 Paris Agreement. In general, there was almost zero percentage interest in "green" IR during the period. IR interest in Ukraine rose to nearly 8% of SSCI articles published in 2023, and IR interest in environmental and climate change remains at about 3–4% of published IR articles. In other words, insignificant.

In contrast to the lack of IR interest in Ukraine, textbooks and courses since the late 1990s have generally had one chapter or one lecture on environmental politics. For example, Matthew Paterson's chapters on green politics in Burchill and Linklater (1996) and Devatak and True (2022), Robyn Eckersley's (latterly with Olaf Corry) chapter on green theory in Dunne, Kurki, Kušić, and Smith (2024), John Vogler's chapter on environmental issues in Baylis, Smith, and Owens (2022), or Cynthia Weber's (2021) chapter on Environmentalism. Uniquely among IR textbooks, Simon Dalby's chapter on nature and Carl Death's chapter on the planet represent two chapters in Edkins and Zehfuss (2018). However, in my experience, no widely-used textbook or widely-taught course has ever taken ecological and climate emergencies seriously by starting a textbook with a framing chapter on the centrality of the environment or ecology as part of a holistic analysis of planetary politics. In this way, the lack of concern for teaching Ukrainian and planetary politics in IR is interwoven—Ukraine can be considered a microcosm in the paradigmatic shift from IR to planetary politics. Just as the peripheralized, marginalized, and colonized subject of Ukraine has not been adequately taught in the IR and EU studies of Western European universities, neither has ecological unsustainability. Clearly other subjects such as the postcolonial world or the non-human world could, and should, be part of genuinely planetary politics.

3. Geopolitics of the 19th Century

> The sides underline that Russia and China, as world powers and permanent members of the United Nations Security Council, intend to firmly adhere to moral principles and accept their responsibility, strongly advocate the international system with the central coordinating role of the United Nations in international affairs, defend the world order based on international law, including the purposes and principles of the Charter of the United Nations, advance multipolarity and promote the democratization of international relations, together create an even more prospering, stable, and just world, jointly build international relations of a new type. (Putin and Xi 2022)

The transformation of teaching, including the elevation of 'geopolitics' during the Russian invasion and Ukrainian counter-offensive, 2022–2025, has focused on the rapid process of re-education and rethinking of teaching on Ukraine and Russia in IR and EU studies courses. The Russia-China Joint Statement on International Relations of 4 February 2022 claimed that the two countries intended to firmly adhere to the moral principles, central coordinating role, and international law of the UN. However, the illegal Russian annexation and human rights abuses in Crimea and parts of Eastern Ukraine since 2014, and Chinese human rights abuses against Uyghurs and other minorities in Xinjiang since 2014, demonstrate the failure to adhere to the moral principles and international law of the UN and the Universal Declaration of Human Rights. Just 20 days later, the Russian invasion of Ukraine and the support of

China ridiculed Putin and Xi's joint declaration. During five votes in the UN General Assembly on 2 March 2022, 24 March 2022, 7 April 2022, 12 October 2022, and 23 February 2023, Russia consistently disregarded and broke the purposes and principles of the Charter of the UN, supported by four other autocracies (Belarus, Eritrea, North Korea, and Syria). China led a group of 30-plus other, largely autocratic countries to abstain from supporting the UN and Ukraine during these votes. In contrast, the purposes and principles of the UN and Ukraine were upheld by the support of 140-plus largely democratic countries during these votes. Thus, while the failure of so many members to defend the principles of the UN and the territorial integrity of Ukraine marked the end of 20th-century IR in 2014, the events of 2022 indicated that many countries were intent on returning to the geopolitics of the 19th century, prior to the establishment of the UN.

From 2021 to 2023, I taught and convened the required first-semester undergraduate/bachelor's course in international politics for approximately 150 Swedish students at Lund University. The course uses the 20th-century conventions of introducing theories and issues and is taught with a combination of a simple Swedish textbook (Gustavson and Tallberg 2021) and a more advanced English textbook (Baylis, Smith, and Owens 2022). After the February 2022 invasion, we were able to adapt the course by adding a new secondary book, Mark Galeotti's (2022) *Putin's Wars: From Chechnya to Ukraine,* to the book review section of the course, as well as introducing the war into the parts of the course on international conflict and international cooperation. These adaptations are clearly similar to so many IR courses and textbooks across Western Europe — existing paradigms and purveyors of IR knowledge remain hegemonic despite the radical transformations of 21st-century IR.

Charts 5 and 6: SSCI references to "International Relations," "Geopolitics," "Multipolar," and "Neoimperial/ Neocolonial"[3] 1990–2023 expressed absolutely and in percentages.

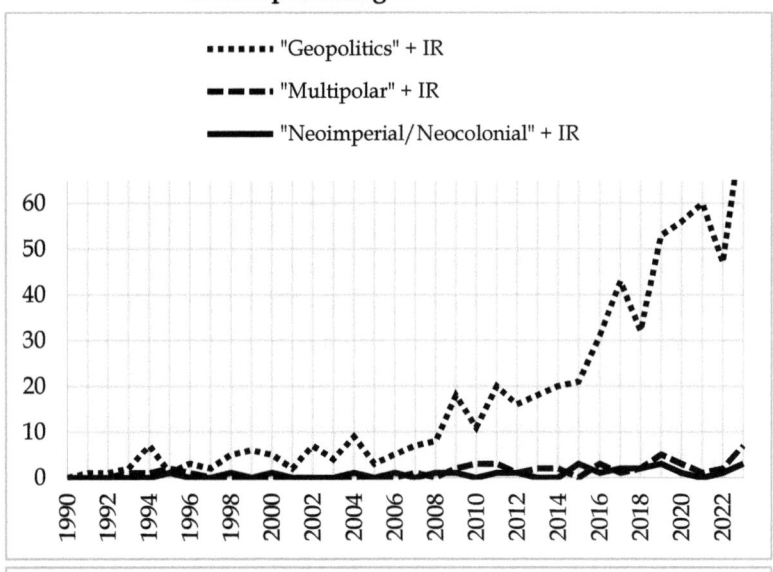

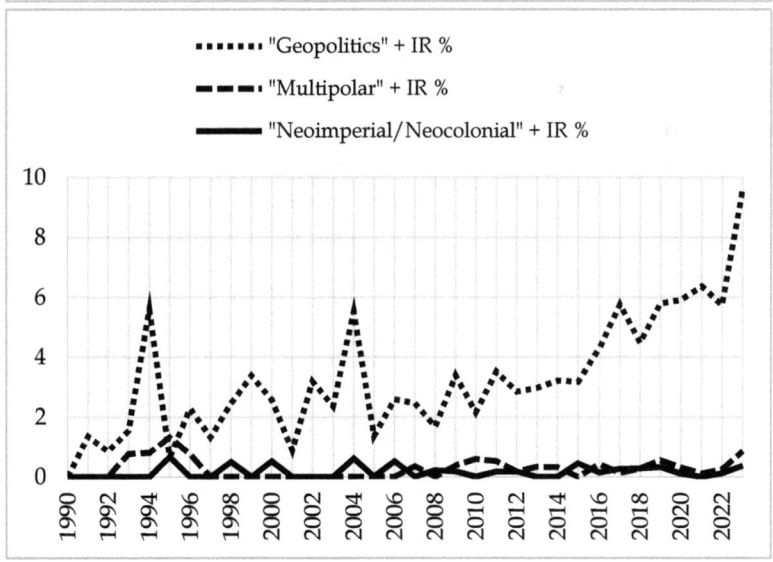

Chart 5 (left) shows the increasing amount of research referring to "International Relations" plus "Geopolitics" from 1990 to 2023, with a more subtle increase in research referring to "Multipolar" and "Neoimperial/Neocolonial." Research referring to "geopolitics" has increased from zero articles in 1990 to 80 articles in 2023. The USA's war on terror, Chinese foreign policy, and the Russian invasion of Ukraine appear to be driving this development. These developments are also reflected in the gradual but more subtle increases in articles referring to "multipolar" and "neoimperial/neocolonial" to describe the rise of the BRICS since the 2007 GFC. Comparing Chart 5 with Chart 1 suggests that while there was a gradual increase in references to geopolitics from 2008 to 2015, the rapid increase in articles referring to geopolitics corresponds to the Russian occupation and invasion of Ukraine from 2014 to 2023. Chart 6 (right) shows the relative use of the phrases "International Relations" plus "Geopolitics," "Multipolar," and "Neoimperial/Neocolonial" as a percentage of the incidence of the phrase "International Relations" from 1990 to 2023. The chart shows how references to geopolitics, and a lesser extent multipolar, were relatively higher after the end of the Cold War (until 2004), then rising again after 2015. The relative patterns for geopolitics, post-2014, are obviously similar to those for Ukraine in charts 1 and 2.

These SSCI results and the survey of recently updated IR textbooks indicate two worrying trends in response to the Russian invasion. First, recently updated IR textbooks, such as Viotti and Kauppi (2023: 229) and Dunne, Kurki, Kušić, and Smith (2024), treat the Russian invasion of Ukraine as a case study in "realism" (Williams 2024, 68). While Baylis, Smith, and Owens (2022) provide a fairer analysis of the invasion in terms of globalization, new world dis-order, rising powers, global security, European integration,

---

3   "Neo-imperial" = ("neo-imperial" OR "neoimperial" OR "neo-imperialism" OR "neoimperialism")
"Neo-colonial" = ("neo-colonial " OR "neocolonial " OR "neo-colonialism" OR "neocolonialism")

global trade and finance, the overall trend is that the Russian invasion can be understood and analyzed in terms of existing IR frameworks. Second, as the increasing amount of IR research referring to geopolitics demonstrates, the invasion is widely seen in conventional IR as part of a geopolitical struggle between global powers of the USA and EU vs. Russia and China.

In contrast to these 19th-century views of geopolitics, the Russian invasion of Ukraine suggests five lessons for teaching a more 21st-century IR that overcomes the "persistence of Cold War binaries" (Pishchikova 2023). First, the Russian invasion must be understood as an act of neoimperialism and neocolonialism rather than being "westsplained" as realist geopolitics (Kurylo 2023; Hendl Burlyuk, O'Sullivan, and Arystanbek 2024). Using Russian neoimperialism to reimpose the imperial Russian empire of 1721-1917 or the Soviet empire of 1917-1991 is the driving force behind Vladimir Putin, including the military interventions in Moldova 1990-1992, Chechnya 1994-1996 and 1999-2009, Georgia 2008, Ukraine 2014 and 2022 (Kuzio 2009; Snyder 2018; Oksamytna 2023). Neocolonialism involves self-identifying ethnic Russians in these countries acting as the colonial rulers of occupied territories such as Transnistria, Chechnya, Abkhazia, South Ossetia, Crimea, and Donbas, which in 2022 led to the "postcolonial moment in Russia's war against Ukraine" (Mälksoo 2023 in Burlyuk and Musliu 2023, 609; also Berglund and Bolkvadze 2024).

Second, the support for the Russian invasion and opposition to the purposes and principles of the UN charter must be understood within the context of a multipolar view of emergent international order with the 'great powers' of the USA, China, Russia, and India dominating. The absurdity of such a limited view of multipolarity in IR is that these four powers currently make up approximately 42% of the world's population and will diminish to approximately 26% of the world's population by 2100 (Vollset et al. 2020). A more accurate reading of this changing world order is that, in general, democracies support, and autocracies oppose, the UN and international rule of law. The UN GA votes on the occupation and invasion of Ukraine demonstrate this reading, with Russia supported by the closed autocracies of Belarus, Cuba, North Korea, and Syria (plus China, Laos, Mali, Nicaragua, Uzbekistan, and Vietnam on one-off votes). In contrast, the UN and Ukraine are supported by 140 states, of which more than 75% are democracies (V-Dem Institute 2024). In this context, the need for support for the UN and the international rule of law in opposition to Russian imperialism was made clearly by Kenyan UN Ambassador Martin Kimani in a speech to the UN Security Council on 21 February 2022:

> Rather than form nations that looked ever backward into history with a dangerous nostalgia, we chose to look forward to a greatness none of our many nations and peoples had ever known. We chose to follow the rules of the OAU and the United Nations Charter not because our borders satisfied us but because we wanted something greater forged in peace.... We further strongly condemn the trend — in the last few decades — of powerful states, including members of this Security Council, breaching International Law with little regard. Multilateralism lies on its deathbed tonight. It has been assaulted, as it has been by other powerful states in the recent past.... Let me conclude by reaffirming Kenya's respect for the territorial integrity of Ukraine within its internationally recognized borders (Kimani 2022; Yakovlyev 2022).

Third, the Russian invasion must be seen as part of a wider campaign of disinformation, gray zones and hybrid warfare involving the state-funded private military company Wagner Group, the Patriot Media Group, the Internet Research Agency, the Russian Institute for Strategic Studies, the Russia Today/RT, Sputnik news agency, and a myriad of state-backed disinformation operations (Khylko 2023; Kormych and Malyarenko 2023; Krainikova and Prokopenko 2023; Solovei 2023). This disinformation and influence campaign began with Putin's appointment in 1999 and stretches across Europe to the USA and from the Middle East to Africa. The campaign has been most successful in undermining democracy in the UK, with highly placed individuals within politics and widespread interference in the 2014 Scottish independence and 2016 EU membership referenda (BREXIT) (Digital, Culture, Media and Sport Committee 2019; Mueller 2019; Intelligence and Security Committee 2020). In addition, the campaign has supported and shaped far-right parties across the EU with 'trojan horse' parties such as UKIP, French National Front/Rally, Alternative for Germany, Italian Northern League, Netherlands Party for Freedom, and Sweden Democrats all serving the interests of Russia (Anton 2022; Oksanen 2015, 2022; Polyakova et al. 2016, 2017, 2018; Shekhovtsov 2023).

Fourth, tragically, the Russian invasion of Ukraine involves four mass atrocity crimes: genocide, war crimes, crimes against humanity, and ethnic cleansing. In March 2022, the International Criminal Court (ICC) opened an investigation into the situation in Ukraine, including war crimes and crimes against humanity or genocide (ICC 2022). Crimes against humanity are the most widespread atrocity, defined as acts "committed as part of a widespread or systematic attack directed against any civilian population" (article 7, ICC 1998: 3-5). In October 2023, the UN Independent International Commission of Inquiry (UN IICI) on Ukraine documented evidence of "indiscriminate attacks by Russian armed forces, which have led to deaths and injuries of civilians and the destruction and damage of civilian objects" (UN IICI 2023: 2). Russian war crimes are equally prevalent, defined as "violations of international humanitarian law (treaty or customary law) that incur individual criminal responsibility under international law… war crimes must always take place in the context of an armed conflict, either international or non-international" (Geneva Conventions 1949; article 8, ICC 1998: 5-10). The UN ICI (2023) collected evidence showing that "Russian authorities have committed the war crimes of willful killing, torture, rape and other sexual violence, and the deportation of children to the Russian Federation." In March 2023, the ICC (2023) issued arrest warrants against Vladimir Putin and Maria Alekseyevna Lvova-Belova over allegations of involvement in the war crime of child abductions during the invasion of Ukraine.

Fifth, in complete contrast to teaching and scholarship on the "post-soviet space," the Ukrainian response to the Russian invasion has demonstrated loudly and clearly across the world the determination and agency of Ukrainians to control their destiny (Kudlenko 2023; Poberezhna, Burlyuk, and van Heelsum 2024). Following the

Maidan Revolution, the Association Agreement between the EU and Ukraine, including a Deep and Comprehensive Free Trade Area, was agreed in 2014 leading to the 2019 amendment of the Constitution of Ukraine aiming to join the EU and NATO. After the Russian invasion, the process of Ukrainian EU membership was accelerated with an application to join in February 2022, leading to the European Council opening accession negotiations in December 2023 (Rabinovych and Pintsch 2024; Noutcheva and Zarembo 2024). Ukraine is not alone in seeking a more secure destiny within European organizations, with Denmark joining the EU's CSDP in 2022, Finland and Sweden joining NATO in 2023 and 2024, and at the same time, Ukraine, Georgia, Bosnia and Herzegovina have all sought greater security within NATO (Wiesner and Knodt 2024; Zarembo 2024).

These five lessons of Russian neoimperialism and neocolonialism, opposition to the purposes and principles of the UN charter, disinformation and manipulation, Russian mass atrocity crimes, and finally, Ukrainian independence and agency all demonstrate the importance of shifting IR teaching away from 19th-century geopolitics and four-power multipolarism, and towards 21st-century planetary politics that escapes the binary paradigm of the past 75 years.

4. Conclusion: Ukraine as a Microcosm of Planetary Politics in the 21st Century

> Chernobyl perhaps marks the start of the wider public awareness of the fragility of the human environment. But even without a Chernobyl or a greenhouse effect, the result of a great lessening of the fear of nuclear war was always likely to be that mankind, the well-off section of it, anyway, would start to concentrate its anxieties on the health of the planet (Woollacott "Planet Politics" 1989).

The necessary paradigm shift to teaching the Russian war against Ukraine and other crises demands new thinking about planetary politics in the 21st century. As Martin Woollacott presciently observed in 1989, the events in Ukrainian Chornobyl marked the start of a wider awareness of the fragility of the human environment, the greenhouse effect, and the health of the planet he called "planet politics." It is only through understanding and coming to terms with the paradigm shift from IR to planetary politics over the past 35 years that it is possible to contribute in a meaningful way to teaching the Russian invasion of Ukraine as a microcosm of planetary politics (Manners 2002: 10; 2008: 37). Fourteen years after Woollacott labeled the era of planetary politics, Karen Litfin (2003: 481) argued that "planetary politics ... are characterized by truly planetary relations of causality that can only be understood and addressed holistically." Planetary politics means that economic, social, ecological, conflictual and political relations and crises cannot be considered independently—they are symbiotic (Manners 2023, 2024a).

The Russian invasion of Ukraine is a microcosm of the wider planetary organic crisis of five symbiotic dimensions of economy, society, ecology, conflict, and polity (Manners 2020, 2024b). Stephen Gill and Solomon Benatar (2020: 171) argue that a planetary organic crisis involves "interacting and deepening structural crises of economy/development, society, ecology, politics, culture and ethics—in ways that are unsustainable." The invasion of Ukraine represents a microcosm of these crises and politics because of the way in which economic (in)equality, social (in)justice, ecological (un)sustainability, conflict (in)security, and political (ir)resilience are symbiotic to understanding both the driving forces and the prospects for Ukraine.

Economically, the Ukrainian and Russian economies both experienced negative growth during the period 1989–1997, but from 1998–2008, the Ukrainian economy outperformed the Russian economy. The GFC had a negative effect on both economies, but the Ukrainian economic downturn in 2014–2015 was particularly bad. The Russian invasion had a destructive effect on the Russian economy, but it was worse for the Ukrainian economy. However, in terms of economic (in)equality, the economies are quite different, with Ukraine having a 0.45 gini income inequality index, broadly comparable to that of the EU, while Russia has an index of 0.60 — one of the worst in the Global North (Alvaredo et al. 2022). The extent to which Russian wealth and inequality are being "sucked up" by wealthy oligarchs surrounding Putin is seen in the dominating role of Russia's ultra-wealthy 1% taking 25% of the national income share, while the Russian super-wealthy 10% take 50% of the national income share. In comparison, Ukraine is broadly in line with EU averages, with the top 1% taking 10–12% of the national income share and the top 10% taking 35% of the national income share.

Socially, the Social Progress Index (SPI) ranks the EU at an average of 44th position out of 170 countries with an index score of 84 on 3 dimensions of basic human needs, foundations of wellbeing, and opportunity (Social Progress Imperative 2024). Ukraine ranks 59th on the SPI with an index score of 70 (up from 66 in 2011), similar to other EU applicants Albania, North Macedonia, Bosnia and Herzegovina. Russia ranks 76th on the SPI with an index score of 67 (down from 68 in 2017), with a fall in opportunity and, most significantly, a collapse in rights and voice since 2011. Changing demographics will be one of the greatest challenges to social justice this century, with the EU 27 population falling from approximately 448 million today to roughly 308 million by 2100 or to approximately 340 million if the EU enlarges to 36 by 2100 (Vollset et al. 2020). Both Russia and Ukraine have low fertility rates, lowered by the invasion and war, which will lead the Russian population to drop from approx. 146 million today to approx. 106 million by 2100, and the Ukrainian population to drop from approx. 41 million today to approx. 18 million by 2100.

Ecologically, the invasion of Ukraine has involved "ecocide" with nuclear power stations such as Chornobyl and Zaporizhzhia put at risk, while munitions and landmines contaminate and condemn fields and forests, dams such as Kakhovka have been destroyed, and rivers such as the Desna poisoned (Yavorska et al. 2024; Shahini et al. 2024). As the world's major exporter of natural gas and second-largest exporter of oil in 2022, Russia is both a 'petrostate' (making up 30–50% of the state budget) and one of the world's worst fossil fuel polluters. Adriana Petryna (2023: 15) argues that the Russian invasion of Ukraine centralizes a range of planetary challenges, including the need for "de-occupation as planetary politics," and shows how "genocide legitimizes both anti-human and anti-planetary violence." As Charts 7 and 8 illustrate below, the study of eco-centric "ecology" rather than the anthropocentric environment in IR only emerged since the 2010 Nagoya Protocol to the Convention on Biological Diversity and the 2015 Paris Agreement. In contrast, the realization of the "climate crisis" and "planetary politics" in IR are far more recent phenomena from 2020 onwards, possibly driven by the COVID-19 pandemic.

Charts 7 and 8: SSCI references to "International Relations," "Ecology,"[4] "Climate Crisis."[5], and "Planetary Politics."[6] 1990–2023 expressed absolutely and in percentages.

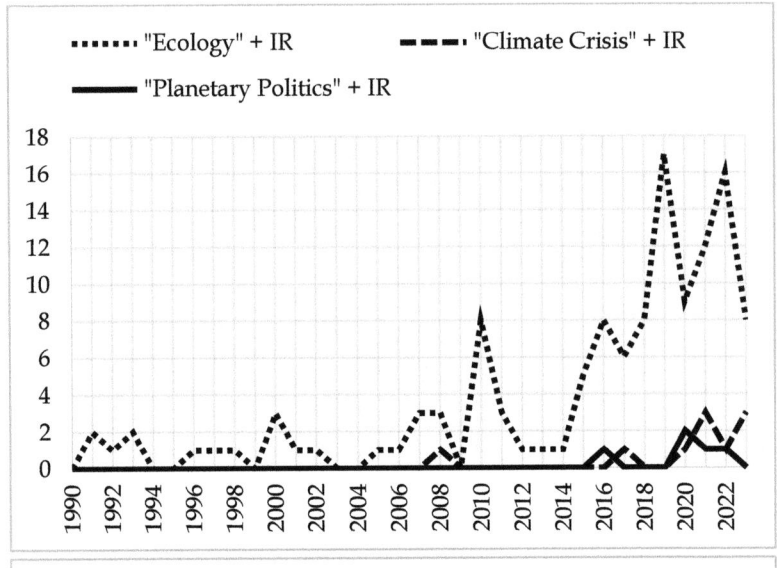

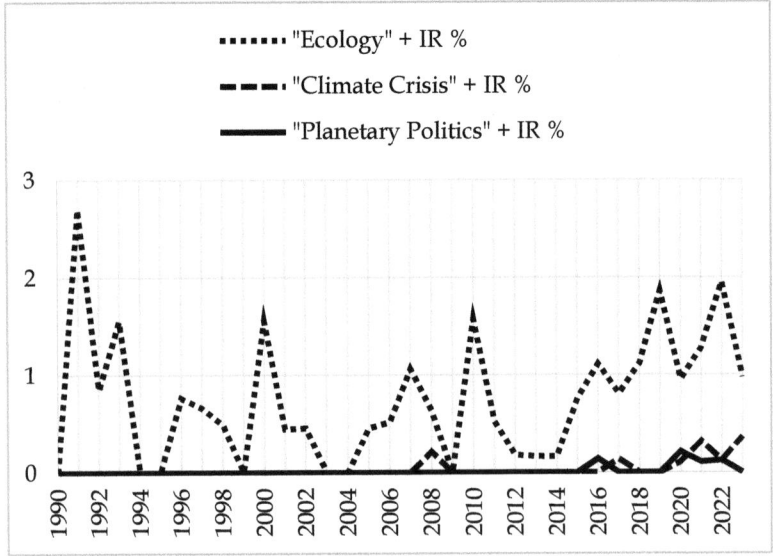

---

4 "Ecology" = "Ecology" OR "Ecological"

Chart 7 (left) shows the slowly increasing amount of research referring to "Ecology" in IR scholarship from 2009 until 2022. However, the amount of ecological IR research is tiny compared to the previous charts, perhaps reflecting psychological climate disavowal (Thierry, Horn, Von Hellermann, and Gardner 2023). In comparison, IR research on the climate crisis/emergency has only begun to emerge since the IPCC AR5 in 2014 and the Paris Agreement in 2015 demonstrated the failure to address the crisis/emergency. The anthropocentrism and egocentrism of contemporary IR scholarship remained hegemonic during the period, with planetary political attempts to escape the paradigm by Karen Litfin (2003), Paul Gilroy (2004), Gayatri Spivak (2003), and Achille Mbembe (2022) barely registering in IR. However, compared to the 400 plus references to environmental IR and 300 plus references to climate change since 2007, the 125 references to ecological IR lie 16 years behind in terms of research and publication.

Chart 8 (right) shows the relative use of the phrases "International Relations" plus "Ecology," "Climate Crisis/Emergency," and "Planetary Politics" as a percentage of the incidence of the phrase "International Relations" from 1990 to 2023. The chart shows how references to ecology have been sporadic since the end of the Cold War. While this pattern is somewhat similar to climate change IR research, the relative levels of research references are about half for ecological research.

In terms of conflict, the Russian invasion of Ukraine is a microcosm of the increasing impunity with which neoimperial great powers take action in multipolar politics. Prior to 2010 interstate conflicts had been slowly falling in number across the world (there was only an interstate conflict between Eritrea and Djibouti during 2004-2010). Since 2010, interstate conflicts in the Middle East, South Asia, Caucasus, and Ukraine have thrown the world back into arms racing, with risks of regional conflict in the Sahel, Palestine,

---

5   "Climate Crisis" = "Climate Crisis" OR "Climate Emergency"
6   "Planetary Politics" = "Planet Politics" OR "Planetary Politics"

Yemen/Iran/Saudi Arabia, Kashmir, the Black Sea, the Baltic, and Taiwan. As Ukrainian scholars of the invasion have made clear, understanding conflict needs far greater knowledge than 'westplaining' the grabbing of territories like a game of *Risk* (Burlyuk and Musliu 2023: 607; Tyushka 2023: 652). As the discussions of economy, society, and ecology suggest, in unequal, unjust, and unsustainable countries such as Russia, the population and civil society are just too weak and fractured to form the foundation of a viable society and oppose the ruling kleptocracy. In this context, neoimperialism and neocolonialism with impunity are the foundation for the governing oligarchy, as Ukrainian scholars know all too well.

Finally, the general culmination of economic inequality, social injustice, ecological unsustainability, and conflict insecurity led to the observation that both freedom and democracy are under threat across the world. The Russian invasion of Ukraine represents a microcosm of this wider pattern, with Russian inequality, injustice, and unsustainability facilitating its aggression and impunity as part of the Russian decline of freedom and democracy. According to Freedom House (2024), the world has now seen 18 years of decline in global freedom, with Russia being at its most free in 1991, remaining "partly free" from 1991–2003, and dropping to "not free" from 2004 to 2024. Similar evidence is presented by the V-Dem Institute (2024), with autocratization continuing to be the dominant trend of the past 15 years. According to V-Dem, Russia was in the "autocratic grey zone" from 1992–1999, then became an "electoral autocracy" from 1999 onwards, where it is currently ranked 159th on the liberal democracy index (out of 179 countries). Thus, the long-term decline in Russian freedom and democracy since 1991 has led to it becoming a "not free" "electoral autocracy" since Putin came to power in 1999.

In contrast, according to Freedom House, Ukraine was "partly free" from 1991–2003, became "free" after the 2005 Orange Revolution between 2005–2010, returned to being "partly free" under Viktor Yanukovych in 2010 and has kept this status ever since. V-

Dem Institute data demonstrates how Ukraine was a form of autocracy between 1991–1993, 1998–2005, 2010–2018, and 2022–2023, and was a form of democracy between 1994–1997, 2006–2009, and 2019–2021, and is currently ranked 109th on the liberal democracy index. What these two sources of data demonstrate is that Russia is an irresilent autocracy without the capacity to recover from elected dictatorship since 1999, while Ukraine is a more resilient polity with the ability to spring back from autocracy to democracy as it did in 1994 (first parliamentary and presidential elections), 2006 (Orange Revolution and election of president Yushchenko), and 2019 (election of president Zelenskyy). Thus, the irresilience and decline of Russian democracy helped fuel its invasion of Ukraine, while the resilience of Ukrainian democracy helped it resist the Russian invasion.

These five dimensions of planetary politics illustrate how Ukraine is a microcosm of larger events but leaves plenty of space for Ukrainian determination and agency. The teaching of the Russian invasion and war against Ukraine must help students and teachers alike to understand the symbiotic relationships between inequality, injustice, unsustainability, insecurity, and resilience in the planetary politics of the 21st century. This article argues that the greatest challenge of teaching IR in the context of the Russian war against Ukraine is that Western IR is stuck in a 20th-century paradigm of thinking. The article then set out how incorporating the war into a first-semester introductory course on international politics initially involved adapting the course to empirical events, such as lectures on conflict and cooperation. However, the war has led to five lessons for rethinking the teaching of neoimperialism and neocolonialism, opposition to the purposes and principles of the UN charter, disinformation and manipulation, Russian mass atrocity crimes, and Ukrainian independence and agency. While the article did not discuss teaching methods and technology (these are covered in Tymofii Brik's chapter), it did demonstrate the need to shift pedagogical paradigms and address the need for Ukrainian knowledge about the war (meaning more information from Ukrainian scholars who are on the 'front line'). In this respect the article used the rich and wide range of Ukrainian scholarship and literature to discuss this knowledge, as the bibliography demonstrates. Finally, the article did not address the emotional and psychological impact of the war on students and staff, which is covered in Galyna Solovei's chapter. However, it is clear from the experience in this volume that the planetary organic crisis is having an increasingly negative effect on the mental health of all involved in the conflict, including the effects of the rise of the Russian far-right autocrats and their neoimperialism, the Russian invasion, and the ecological and climate catastrophe in which Ukraine is a Microcosm.

References

Alvaredo, Facundo, Atkinson, Anthony, Piketty, Thomas, and Saez, Emmanuel. (2022) *World Inequality Database*. Paris: World Inequality Lab. http://wid.world/data

Anton, Wiebke. (2022) *"Russia" in the European Parliament: Voting Patterns, Discourse-Coalitions and Self-Other Representations*. Munich: Ludwig-Maximilians-University.

Baylis, John, and Smith, Steve. (eds.) (1997) *The Globalization of World Politics: An Introduction to International Relations*. Oxford: Oxford University Press.

Baylis, John, Smith, Steve, and Owens, Patricia. (eds.) (2022) *The Globalization of World Politics: An Introduction to International Relations*, 9th edn. Oxford: Oxford University Press.

Berenskötter, Felix. (2018) "E pluribus unum? How textbooks cover theories," in Gofas, Andreas, Hamati-Ataya, Inanna, and Onuf, Nicholas (Eds.) *Sage Handbook of History, Philosophy and Sociology of International Relations*. London: Sage, 446-68.

Berglund, Christofer, and Bolkvadze, Ketevan. (2024) "Sons of the Soil or Servants of the Empire? Profiling the Guardians of Separatism in Abkhazia and South Ossetia," *Problems of Post-Communism* 71(1): 37-48.

Bretherton, Charlotte, and Vogler, John. (1999) *The European Union as a Global Actor*. London: Routledge.

Brown, Chris. (1997) *Understanding International Relations*. Basingstoke: Macmillan.

Burchill, Scott, and Linklater, Andrew. (eds.) (1996) *Theories of International Relations*. Basingstoke: Macmillan.

Burlyuk, Olga, and Musliu, Vjosa. (2023) "The Responsibility to Remain Silent? On the Politics of Knowledge Production, Expertise and (Self-) Reflection in Russia's War against Ukraine," *Journal of International Relations and Development* 26(4): 605-18.

Devetak, Richard, and True, Jacqui. (2022) *Theories of International Relations*, 6th edn. London: Bloomsbury.

Digital, Culture, Media and Sport Committee. (2019) *Disinformation and "Fake News"*, House of Commons (2017-19, HC 1791), 18 February.

Dunne, Tim, Kurki, Milja, Kušić, Katarina, and Smith, Steve. (eds.) (2024) *International Relations Theories: Discipline and Diversity*, 6th edn. Oxford: Oxford University Press.

Edkins, Jenny, and Zehfuss, Maja. (eds.) (2018) *Global Politics: A New Introduction*, 3rd edn. London: Routledge.

Freedom House. (2024) *Freedom in the World 2024: The Mounting Damage of Flawed Elections and Armed Conflict*. Washington DC: Freedom House.

Galeotti, Mark. (2022) *Putin's Wars: From Chechnya to Ukraine*. Oxford: Osprey Publishing.

Geneva Conventions. (1949) *Four Geneva Conventions and three Protocols on the treatment of soldiers, prisoners of war and non-combatants during wartime, 1949, 1977, and 2005*. Switzerland: International Committee of the Red Cross.

Gill, Stephen, and Benatar, Solomon. (2020) "Reflections on the Political Economy of Planetary Health," *Review of International Political Economy* 27(1): 167-90.

Gilroy, Paul. (2004) *After Empire: Melancholia or Convivial Culture?* Abingdon: Routledge.

Gustavsson, Jakob, and Tallberg, Jonas. (eds.) (2021) *Internationella relationer*. Lund: Studentlitteratur.

Hendl, Tereza, Burlyuk, Olga, O'Sullivan, Mila, and Arystanbek, Aizada. (2024) "(En)Countering Epistemic Imperialism: A Critique of 'Westsplaining' and Coloniality in Dominant Debates on Russia's Invasion of Ukraine," *Contemporary Security Policy* 45(2): 171-209.

Intelligence and Security Committee. (2020) *Russia Report*, House of Commons (2017-2019, HC 632) 21 July.

International Criminal Court. (1998) *Rome Statute adopted by the United Nations Diplomatic Conference of Plenipotentiaries on the Establishment of an International Criminal Court*, 17 July.

International Criminal Court. (2022) "Situation in Ukraine," ICC-01/22, 2 March. https://www.icc-cpi.int/situations/ukraine

International Criminal Court. (2023) "Situation in Ukraine: ICC judges issue arrest warrants against Vladimir Vladimirovich Putin and Maria Alekseyevna Lvova-Belova," Press Release: 17 March. https://www.icc-cpi.int/news/situation-ukraine-icc-judges-issue-arrest-warrants-against-vladimir-vladimirovich-putin-and

Khylko, Olena. (2023) "Resilience-Building in Grey Security Zone Countries," *Scientific Collection «InterConf+»* 34(159): 37-48.

Kimani, Martin. (2022) "Statement during the UN SC Meeting on the Situation in Ukraine," Permanent Mission of the Republic of Kenya, 21 February.

Kormych, Borys, and Malyarenko, Tetyana. (2023) "From Gray Zone to Conventional Warfare: the Russia-Ukraine Conflict in the Black Sea," *Small Wars & Insurgencies* 34(7): 1235-70.

Krainikova, Tetiana, and Prokopenko, Serhii. (2023) "Waves of Disinformation in the Hybrid Russian-Ukrainian War," *Current Issues of Mass Communication* 33: 12-25.

Kudlenko, Anastasiia. (2023) "Roots of Ukrainian Resilience and the Agency of Ukrainian Society Before and After Russia's Full-Scale Invasion," *Contemporary Security Policy* 44(4): 513-29.

Kurylo, Bohdana. (2023) "The Ukrainian Subject, Hierarchies of Knowledge Production and the Everyday: An Autoethnographic Narrative," *Journal of International Relations and Development* 26(4): 685-97.

Kuzio, Taras. (2009) "Strident, Ambiguous and Duplicitous: Ukraine and the 2008 Russia-Georgia War," *Demokratizatsiya* 17(4): 350-72.

Litfin, Karen. (2003) "Planetary Politics," in Agnew, John, Mitchell, Katharyne, and Toal, Gerard. (eds.) A *Companion to Political Geography*. Oxford: Blackwell, 470–82.

McCormick, John. (1999) *Understanding the European Union: A Concise Introduction*. Basingstoke: Macmillan.

Mälksoo, Maria. (2023) "The Postcolonial Moment in Russia's War against Ukraine," *Journal of Genocide Research* 25(3-4): 471-81.

Manners, Ian. (1999) "The European Union and Moldova Beyond the PCA," in Bruton, Leilah (ed.) *The Republic of Moldova: Time for a New EU Strategy?* Brussels: Stiftung Wissenschaft und Politik, 57-77.

Manners, Ian. (2002) *European [security] Union: from existential threat to ontological security*, COPRI working paper 5 (Copenhagen: Copenhagen Peace Research Institute). https://portal.research.lu.se/files/108768568/Ian_Manners_2002_European_security_Union_from_existential_threat_to_ontological_security_COPRI_5.pdf

Manners, Ian. (2009) "The Normative Power of the European Union in a Globalised World," in Laïdi, Zaki (ed.) *EU Foreign Policy in a Globalized World: Normative Power and Social Preferences*. London: Routledge, 23-37.

Manners, Ian. (2010) "As You Like It: European Union Normative Power in the European Neighbourhood Policy," in Whitman, Richard, and Wolff, Stefan (eds.) *The European Neighbourhood Policy in Perspective: Context, Implementation and Impact*. Basingstoke: Palgrave Macmillan, 29-50.

Manners, Ian. (2018) "Political Psychology of European Integration: The (Re)production of Identity and Difference in the Brexit Debate," *Political Psychology* 39(6): 1213-32.

Manners, Ian. (2020) "European Communion and Planetary Organic Crisis," in Brack, Nathalie, and Gürkan, Seda (eds.) *Theorising the Crises of the European Union*. London: Routledge, 159-82.

Manners, Ian. (2023) "Planetary Politics in the Twenty-Second Century." in Horn, Laura, Mert, Ayşem, and Müller, Franziska. (eds.) *The Palgrave Handbook of Global Politics in the 22nd Century*. Cham: Springer International Publishing, 271-90.

Manners, Ian. (2024a) "Arrival of Normative Power in Planetary Politics," *Journal of Common Market Studies* 62(3): 825-844.

Manners, Ian. (2024b) "Normative Power in the Planetary Organic Crisis," *Cooperation and Conflict* 59. https://doi.org/10.1177/0010836724124454

Mbembe, Achille. (2022) "How to Develop a Planetary Consciousness," *Noema Magazine*, 11 January. https://www.noemamag.com/how-to-develop-a-planetary-consciousness/

Mearsheimer, John, and Rosato, Sebastian. (2023) *How States Think: The Rationality of Foreign Policy*. New Haven, CT: Yale University Press.

Mueller, Robert. (2019) *Report on The Investigation into Russian Interference in the 2016 Presidential Election*. Washington: US Department of Justice, 18 April.

Noutcheva, Gergana, and Zarembo, Kateryna. (2024) "Normative Power at its Unlikeliest: EU Democratic Norms and Security Service Reform in Ukraine," *Cooperation and Conflict* 59. https://doi.org/10.1177/00108367241244978

Nugent, Neil. (1994) *The Government and Politics of the European Union*, 3rd edn. Basingstoke: Macmillan.

Oksamytna, Kseniya. (2023) "Imperialism, Supremacy, and the Russian Invasion of Ukraine," *Contemporary Security Policy* 44(4): 497-512.

Oksanen, Patrik. (2015) "Russia-index: 11 new EU-sceptic parties added," 10 January. https://eublogg.wordpress.com/2015/01/10/russia-index-11-new-eu-sceptic-parties-added/

Oksanen, Patrik. (2022) "SD:s rysslandsröster i Europaparlamentet sticker ut," Säkerhetsrådet, Frivärld, 7 September. https://frivarld.se/sakerhetsradet/sds-rysslandsroster-sticker-ut-i-europaparlamentet/

Petryna, Adriana. (2023) "De-Occupation as Planetary Politics: On the Russian War in Ukraine," *American Ethnologist* 50(1): 10-18.

Poberezhna, Anastasiia, Burlyuk, Olga, and van Heelsum, Anja. (2024) "A Superhero Army, a Courageous People and an Enchanted Land: Wartime Political Myths and Ontological Security in the 2022 Russian Invasion of Ukraine," *Czech Journal of International Relations* 59(1): 59–92.

Polyakova, Alina, Laruelle, Marlene, Meister, Stefan, and Barnett, Neil. (2016) *The Kremlin's Trojan Horses: Russian Influence in France, Germany, and the United Kingdom.* Washington DC: Atlantic Council.

Polyakova, Alina, Kounalakis, Markos, Klapsis, Antonis, Germani, Luigi Sergio, Iacoboni, Jacopo, de Borja Lasheras, Francisco, and de Pedro, Nicolás. (2017) *The Kremlin's Trojan Horses 2.0: Russian influences in Greece, Italy, and Spain.* Washington DC: Atlantic Council.

Polyakova, Alina, Splidsboel-Hansen, Flemming, van Der Noordaa, Robert, Bogen, Øystein, Sundbom, Henrik. (2018) *The Kremlin's Trojan Horses 3.0: Russian influences in Denmark, the Netherlands, Norway, and Sweden.* Washington DC: Atlantic Council.

Pishchikova, Katerina. (2023) "What Ukraine Teaches Us About International Relations and Vice Versa," *Interdisciplinary Political Studies* 9(2): 97-107.

Putin, Vladimir, and Xi, Jinping. (2022) "Joint Statement of the Russian Federation and the People's Republic of China on the International Relations Entering a New Era and the Global Sustainable Development," Beijing, 4 February.

Rabinovych, Maryna, and Pintsch, Anne. (2024) "From the 2014 Annexation of Crimea to the 2022 Russian War on Ukraine: Path Dependence and Socialization in the EU–Ukraine Relations," *Journal of Common Market Studies*. https://doi.org/10.1111/jcms.13572

Scholte, Jan Aarte. (2000) *Globalization: A Critical Introduction.* Basingstoke: Macmillan.

Shahini, Ermir, Shebanina, Olena, Kormyshkin, Iurii, Drobitko, Antonina, and Chernyavskaya, Natalya. (2024) "Environmental Consequences for the World of Russia's war against Ukraine," *International Journal of Environmental Studies* 81(1): 463-474.

Shekhovtsov, Anton. (2023) *Russian Political Warfare: Essays on Kremlin Propaganda in Europe and the Neighbourhood, 2020-2023*. Hannover: Ibidem Press.

Snyder, Timothy. (2018) *The Road to Unfreedom: Russia, Europe, America*. New York: Tim Duggan Books.

Social Progress Imperative. (2024) *2024 Social Progress Index*. Washington, DC: Social Progress Imperative. www.socialprogress.org

Solovei, Galyna. (2023) "Russian Myths of 'One People' and 'NATO's Attack on Russia' in the Legitimization of the Russo-Ukrainian War," in Catalan-Matamoros, Daniel (ed.) *Disinformation and Fact-Checking in Contemporary Society*. Madrid: Dykinson, 101-16.

Spivak, Gayatri. (2003) *Death of a Discipline*. New York: Columbia University Press.

Stein, Janice Gross. (2008) "Foreign Policy Decision-Making: Rational, Psychological, and Neurological Methods," in Smith, Steve, Hadfield, Amelia, and Dunne, Timothy (eds.) *Foreign Policy: Theories, Actors, Cases*, 3rd edn. Oxford: Oxford University Press, 130-46

Thierry, Aaron, Horn, Laura, von Hellermann, Pauline, and Gardner, Charlie. (2023) "'No Research on a Dead Planet': Preserving the Socio-Ecological Conditions for Academia," *Frontiers in Education* 8. https://doi.org/10.3389/feduc.2023.1237076

Tyushka, Andriy. (2023) "In 'Crisis' We Trust? On (Un)Intentional Knowledge Distortion and the Exigency of Terminological Clarity in Academic and Political Discourses on Russia's War against Ukraine," *Journal of International Relations and Development* 26(4): 643-59.

United Nations General Assembly Resolution. (2014) Resolution 68/262, "Territorial Integrity of Ukraine," adopted by the sixty-eighth session of the United Nations General Assembly, 27 March.

United Nations Independent International Commission of Inquiry. (2023) Inquiry on Ukraine pursuant to Human Rights Council resolution 52/32, A/78/540. Geneva: UN Human Rights Council.

V-Dem Institute. (2024) *Democracy Report 2024: Democracy Winning and Losing at the Ballot*. Gothenburg: V-Dem Institute.

Viotti, Paul, and Kauppi, Mark. (2023) *International Relations Theory*, 7th edn. Harlow: Pearson.

Vollset, Stein Emil, *et al.* (2020) "Fertility, mortality, migration, and population scenarios for 195 countries and territories from 2017 to 2100: a forecasting analysis for the Global Burden of Disease Study," *The Lancet* 396(10258): 1285-306.

Wallace, Helen, and Wallace, William. (eds.) (1996) *Policy-Making in the European Union*, 3rd edn. Oxford: Oxford University Press.

Weber, Cynthia. (2021) *International Relations Theory: A Critical Introduction*, 5th edn. Abingdon: Routledge.

Wiesner, Claudia, and Knodt, Michèle. (eds.) (2024) *The War Against Ukraine and the EU: Facing New Realities*. Cham: Springer Nature.

Williams, Michael. (2024) "Classical Realism," in Dunne, Tim, Kurki, Milja, Kušić, Katarina, and Smith, Steve. (eds.) *International Relations Theories: Discipline and Diversity*, 6th edn. Oxford: Oxford University Press, 55-71.

Woollacott, Martin (1989) "The Year Ahead: Planet Politics - Why 1989 Could and Should be a Year of Miracles," *The Guardian*, 2 January.

Yakovlyev, Maksym (2022) "European Imperialism and Colonialism in Africa: Conceptual Lessons for Understanding the Former Soviet Union and Present-Day Russia," *African Journal of Economics, Politics and Social Studies* 1(1): 31-39.

Yavorska, Victoria, Oleksii Buriachenko, Liudmyla Vasechko, Valerii Shapoval, Oleksii Vasechko, and Roman Yedeliev (2024) "Examining the International Political and Legal Accountability of States for Genocide, Ecocide, and Weapons of Mass Destruction: Current Norms, Practices, and Political Implications", *Multidisciplinary Science Journal* 6, 2024ss0739. https://doi.org/10.31893/multiscience.2024ss0739

Zarembo, Kateryna (2024) "Still Normative Power Europe? The Perception of the EU in Ukraine Amidst the Russian War of Aggression", in Claudia Wiesner and Michèle Knodt (eds.) *The War Against Ukraine and the EU: Facing New Realities*. Cham: Springer Nature, 189-206.

Eastern Europe Marginalized in Teaching IR Lessons Learned from Russia's War Against Ukraine

Olena Khylko

Introduction

Wartimes and crises force a reconsideration of existing teaching patterns and approaches, as well as questioning the added value of the knowledge and skills every teacher can equip the students with for their future professional resilience. While crises bring about emotional lability for both sides — teachers and students — they are followed by cognitive and epistemological needs. Against this background, the role of teaching IR courses adequately reflecting on the dynamic nature of the field puts exclusive responsibility on the shoulders of professors, authors and publishers who recommend reading for students gaining tertiary education. Being both ontological and epistemological cornerstones for understanding IR, the theories of IR courses are, at the same time, the least dynamic and open to changes coming from empirical experience, to which wars and conflicts belong. The third year of Russia's invasion of Ukraine is quite a short time for shaking IR theories and teaching them to students, but still enough to make interim conclusions about their deficiencies.

From this angle, this chapter aims to look closer at changes that might be brought to teaching IR studies and IR theories stemming from the experience of the war and Ukraine's resilience. The research will look at and compare the IR curricula and syllabi at leading Western schools from the period preceding the Russian invasion of 2022 and afterward. We will start with an assessment of how the war tested the validity of the mainstream theories dominating in the IR studies, proceed to show the place of Ukraine and the Eastern European region in the dichotomy of theorizing IR and area studies, analyze the trends in the syllabi of IR theories and adjacent courses and substantiate the rationale for embedding the empirical potential of the war into postcolonial theoretical approaches, the attractiveness of which lies in a rich potential for alternative explanations in IR (Mälksoo 2021, 6).

Despite the declared 'end of IR theories' (Dunne, Hansen & Wight 2013), they have rich potential for explaining the relationship between actors and the organization of the world political process. They empower IR studies by making them "theory-led, theory-literate and theory-concerned" (Dunne, Hansen & Wight 2013). IR theories, being a part of IR studies' intellectual structure (Wæver & Tickner 2013) or a "sort of codification of political practice" (Buzan 2018, 394), perform explanatory and constitutive functions (Smith 1995, 27-28) which fulfill the crucial role of a more time-independent intellectual education and allows to reflect on changing challenges (Guzzini 2001, 99).

IR theories have traditionally focused on the explanatory potential of the mainstream theories elaborated by the Western, predominantly Anglo-American scholarship. Still, in 1993, Alfredo C. Robles, Jr. (526-527) wrote that "parochialism still holds sway in the teaching of IR," emphasizing that 80% of all the referencing made in US IR academia belonged to US scholars. Shaken by the decolonization discourse (Davis A. et al. 2020; Hassan and Sajjad 2022; Tucker 2018), IR theories courses very slowly and reluctantly start including into the syllabi the works of non-Western scholars — advanced/critical/postcolonial theories of IR rather than introductory courses to IR. Still, even these modest attempts to make IR studies truly global (Acharya 2014) reflect an ignorance of the explanatory potential of Eastern European empirical material for enriching and complementing IR theories.

This epistemic injustice is addressed by current research, which suggests including Eastern European post- and neocolonial experience in courses or modules on postcolonial theories in IR. This will contribute to re-centering IR and their pluralization shifts (Tickner 2013; Acharya Buzan 2017) by leveraging up non-core or local knowledge and making it more meaningful for IR studies (Kaczmarska 2020). It aims to contribute to the restorative and inclusionary epistemic justice (Hutchings 2023), revealing the silencing of voices outside Eurocentrism (Zondi 2016) and showing the added value of the region's states and Ukraine's experience, in particular, for IR studies teaching. Such inclusion could activate the capacity of integrative pluralism (Dunne 2013, 406), which empowers a theory with added value and with organizational tools to distinguish what is important and what is not and to specify the relations between the factors deemed to be important (Dunne 2013, 410).

IR theories as core intellectual structures in IR studies: deficiencies revealed by the war

The devastating demographic and environmental consequences, scope and declared goals of Russian military intervention in Ukraine (Manners 2024, 840) in 2022 as well as the desperation of Ukraine's resistance, raised questions about the deficiencies of the mainstream IR theoretical paradigms (Dutkiewicz and Smolenski 2023) in comprehending regional (inter)dependencies, interactions, motivations for behavior and decision-making by local actors, as well as in predicting hazardous scenarios that go beyond conventional paradigms and mindsets. This section will indicate several significant vulnerabilities in the dominant IR theories that need to be addressed and compensated by other approaches or theories.

Proponents of the realist paradigm—with its penchant for "great power narcissism" (Hagström 2021) and corresponding marginalization of the agency of small and medium powers—claim the West's responsibility for Russia's aggression against Ukraine (Mearsheimer 2014; Walt 2022) and insist that it was the promise of NATO membership to Kyiv given at the 2008 Bucharest Summit that provoked Moscow (Mearsheimer 2014). However, this stance omits the fact that Vladimir Putin's revisionist speech at the 2007 Munich Security Conference took place before the Bucharest Summit—an important aspect highlighted by Joseph Nye (2022b).

Moreover, in 2000, long before the Bucharest Summit, the updated text of the Foreign Policy Concept of the Russian Federation indicated Moscow's dissatisfaction with the existing world order, claiming that "calculations related to the formation of new equal, mutually beneficial, partnership relations between Russia and the outside world did not materialise" (2000). Among main foreign policy goals, the Concept pointed out strengthening Russia's position "as a great power and as one of the influential centres of the modern world" (Foreign Policy Concept of the Russian Federation 2000) — the goal for which Russia needed Ukraine to get "a critical mass" as Putin believed (Trenin 2013). Amid Russia's intention to strengthen its geopolitical posture, keeping Ukraine in the 'grey zone' without appropriate security guarantees could hardly be considered a reliable option, even from the point of view of realists (Khylko 2017).

Realists downplay the effect domestic politics produce on foreign policy decisions, a true belief that "the pressures of [international] competition weigh more heavily than ideological preferences or internal political pressures" (Waltz 1986, 329), criticized by opponents (Snyder 2013; Shultz 2013) who stressed the significance of parochial interests of elites and institutional factors, hampered analysis of Russian authoritarian political regime specifics as well as domestic changes in Ukraine. The latter were brought partially by approximation with the EU and partially by depriving Russia of its agents of influence that were seeking permanent destabilization.

Neoliberals, in their turn, for decades have believed that the democratization of Russia could be a precondition for a transformative process that would render conflicts inexpedient (Bouchet 2015; Gat 2005). They assumed that economic interdependence in a highly globalized world made wars too expensive, which should deter countries from taking an aggressive stance (Copeland 1996). Following this logic, it would be highly disadvantageous for Russia to start a war, as its economic wellbeing depended heavily on trade with the EU, a key buyer of its energy resources, and the development of the Russian economy was strongly dependent on Western technologies. However, the invasion of Ukraine has shown that rational economic considerations like the impact of the sanctions do not always prevail over other motivations. As Joseph Nye notes, "While economic interdependence can raise the costs of war, it clearly does not prevent it" (2022a).

The preoccupation of realists with the Cold War's great powers' rivalry and the pursuit of power maximization hampered their insightfulness in analyzing specifics and motivations of Russia's policies in the Eastern European region and specifically in Ukraine. At the same time, neoliberals overestimated the ability of interdependence to bring competitors closer together and overlooked the importance of other reasons shaping the policies of regional actors. For both realists and neoliberals, Eastern Europe, apart from Russia, "has generally appeared as an object of projecting power and visions of governance rather than a subject in its own right in the field of making, and making sense of, international relations," as Maria Mälksoo notes (2021, 871).

Constructivists provide fertile ground to comprehend certain motivations for Russia's behavior that are beyond the paradigms of realism and liberalism. As Alexander Wendt argued in 1992, power politics is not a naturally predefined mode of interaction between states but a socially constructed reality that the states continue to reproduce (1992). Based on constructivism ideas, researchers contend that rational choice models are insufficient for exhaustive explanations of Russian behavior, in which perceptions of interest and security are interlinked with its "alternative identities," built around notions of Russia "as a supranational entity or region, understood in cultural civilisationist terms, or in geoeconomic terms—or both at the same time" (Kazharski 2019, 190).

Still, despite the valuable insights on Russia's behavior provided by constructivist notions of interests being shaped by identities, the ruthlessness of the Russian invasion of Ukraine in 2022, as well as the resoluteness of Ukraine's resistance, encouraged an expansion of the range of IR paradigms to understand these events and the preconditions that led to them. In this regard, the ongoing discussions on the need for the decolonization of IR (Davis A. et al. 2020; Hassan and Sajjad 2022; Tucker 2018) inspired renewed attempts to apply a postcolonial lens to the study of the Eastern European region in general and the Russia invasion in particular. Unlike the 1990s and 2000s, when the study of postcolonialism in Russia–Ukraine relations was mainly focused on cultural issues (e.g., see Pavlyshyn 1993), this time, the postcolonial lens is proposed for the entire complex of interactions. This intention was additionally stimulated when Yale University professor Timothy Snyder clearly stated that the Russian war in Ukraine is "a colonial war" and that "Ukraine is a post-colonial country" (2022). The postcolonial and imperial nature constituted by Russia's war against Ukraine was also stressed by other Ukrainian and Western scholars (Burlyuk and Musliu 2023, 606). This marks a significant shift in academic discourse, as Ukraine has long been "among the most flagrantly neglected cases of Soviet colonialism due to the allegedly insufficient applicability of the label 'postcolonial' to the former Soviet/Russian imperial space" (Mälksoo 2023, 473).

Paradoxically, at first glance, the strengthening of neo-colonialist tendencies in the politics of the Russian Federation in the 2010s intensified the academic discourse representing Russia itself as an object of Western colonization, a "European colony" and "subaltern empire" that invaded Ukraine driven by "defensive logic" feeling "threatened by what it perceives is an expansion of the Western empire" (Morozov 2015, 135, 167). Tamar Koplatadze argues that this tendency is largely rooted in the peculiar theoretical discourse on Russia's subaltern and internally colonized identity vis-à-vis the West and that "within this narrative, the Russian Empire and the Soviet Union are regarded as non-colonial powers since the Russian population allegedly suffered more under Russo-Soviet rule than non-Russian nationalities in the annexed territories" (2022). Vera Tolz and Stephen Hutchings note that narratives of Western colonialism and victimization of Russia, echoing the nineteenth-century Slavophiles and early-twentieth-century Eurasianists, became widespread not only in Russia but also among Western left-wing groups and wider non-Western audiences (2023). Andrey Makarychev and Ryhor Nizhnikau argue that "Russia actively utilizes the Western academic rules for its own benefit," mimicking the major vocabularies and redeploying dominant narratives to support the Kremlin propaganda "through Russia-sympathetic scholars" (2023). Inscribed in IR syllabi (e.g., Georgetown University 2020), the respective sources contribute to the further marginalization of Ukraine and the victimization of Russia.

At the same time, the application of postcolonial approaches from the Ukrainian perspective remains less visible that is considered by Bohdana Kurylo as a "refusal to recognise the Ukrainian subject as a legitimate knowledge generator and an agent of its own liberation from Russian colonialism" (2023). Victoria Donovan stresses that Western decolonial discourse "in fact reproduce(s) the same hierarchies of authority and power," continuing to speak "on behalf of' the marginalized others, including Ukrainians" (2023, 169). Vitaly Chernetsky notes that Ukraine's subaltern and marginalized position is "also reflected in the similarly subaltern and marginalized position of Ukrainian studies vis-a-vis Russian studies in the West" (2003, 36-37).

This fits in the general trend of objectifying the countries of Eastern Europe in IR studies (Davis N. 2022; Dudko 2023) and "Western epistemic practices of marginalization and silencing of the CEE Subaltern/Other" sometimes referred to as 'westsplaining' (O'Sullivan and Krulišová 2023). Aliaksei Kazharski points out that the Western discourse on Central and Eastern Europe suffers from "distortions caused by its deep Russo-centrism" and the "assumption that powerful players can and should talk to Moscow over the heads of Central and Eastern European countries" (2022). Such epistemic imperialism leads to the domination of the outsider narratives about what Ukraine is, "often wholly skipping the knowledge produced in Ukraine, by Ukrainians, or by those who study Ukraine specifically," stresses Maria Sonevytsky (2022, 22). Míla O'Sullivan and Kateřina Krulišová point out that, inter alia, the

"Western practices of exclusion of those directly impacted by Russian imperial aggression" and "speaking over Ukraine" contributed to misunderstandings about the imperial nature of the Russian invasion (2023).

For the purposes of teaching IR, we consider such potential of postcolonialism valuable for providing alternative interpretations rooted in justice and the adoption of alternative norms (Wilkens 2017), challenging rationalist notions of power as a tool constraining self-determination (Fanon 1963, 146; Bhabha 1994, 20); explaining the sophisticated connection between memory, historical experiences, and politics, offering insights into the motivations behind resistance and patterns of transformation as vehicles for emancipation. Moreover, it exposes the legacies of colonial rule and imperial administration that inform contemporary global politics (Küçük 2022, 157). Given its ethical underpinnings, postcolonialism offers a promising lens for analyzing the actions of small and medium powers, often marginalized by realists. The study of colonial practices is essential for understanding how these practices have influenced societal responses to domination and shaped various forms of resistance.

Exclusionary practices in teaching IR Studies. Positioning Ukraine and Eastern European region in IR studies.

Superiority and centrality of the West in IR studies (Sanjay Seth 2021; Acharya and Buzan 2007; Malksoo 2021) determined the way IR teaching was organized. A discussion about decolonizing IR and enriching it with non-Western experience was initiated by Hoffman (Hoffmann 1977) and went on for almost 50 years, aiming to deconstruct the modern architecture of knowledge (Tlostanova, Mignolo 2012). As Arlene Tickner writes, "Twenty-five years after Stanley Hoffmann's critical depiction of IR as an American social science, the basic contours of IR have changed surprisingly little. IR textbooks continue to be written by American authors and rely upon

'Americano-centric' representations of global politics in which the United States is normally at the core of world events" (Tickner 2013, 297).

A decolonial approach to IR begins with acknowledging that "entrenched and deeply rooted social and political hierarchies based on exclusionary practices shape both geopolitics and the production of knowledge" (Adamson 2020, 131; Tickner & Wæver 2009; Acharya 2014). Decoloniality, in its turn, "de-normalized the normative, problematized default positions, debunks the a-perspectival, destabilizes the structure, and as a programme to rehabilitate epistemic formations that continue to be repressed under coloniality" (Gallien 2020, 28).

Thus, reasoning for attributing Ukraine, as well as an entire EE region (excluding Russia), to a peripheral knowledge represented as lacking its own epistemological value owing to being perceived as a subordinate and complementary source of knowledge (Wolff 1994; Todorova 1997; Said 1979) is deeply rooted in IR studies and teaching, mainly in the colonial architecture of IR knowledge as well as in a dichotomy of IR theorizing and area studies. Another reason for a 'low-profile' epistemological interest is rooted in the liminality of Ukraine and the Eastern European region on the academic mental map. Ukraine and the region are neither 'West' nor 'non-West,' neither 'Global North' nor 'Global South' (Acharya and Buzan 2010). 'Global East' was invented to compensate for a lack of attribution and recognition for those who do not belong anywhere. Thus, the region experienced 'dual exclusion' by Müller, i.e., was sidelined in current debates about the revalidation of Southern knowledge while also not included in imaginaries of a Global North (Müller 2020, 738). Mälksoo proves broader Eastern European representation as peripheral knowledge in IR manifested by the underrepresentation of EE scholars in most influential academic institutions and journals as well as by representing the states of the region as "mute objects, utilised simply for testing the validity of theoretical elaborations advanced by scholars in the West" (Mälksoo 2021, 19).

In 2014, Acharya, appealing to the global IR establishment, among other dimensions of this phenomenon named "commitment to pluralistic universalism," "redefining existing IR theories and methods and building new ones from societies hitherto ignored as sources of IR knowledge, integrating the study of regions and regionalisms into the central concerns of IR," and "recognizing a broader conception of agency" (Acharya 2014). This research addresses the validity of Acharya's claims and shows how teaching IR reflected these appeals to improve what does not work in IR studies. It contributes to a discussion about the "abundant westernization of the field but about its pluralization with the inclusion of what was not initially there" (Dunne 2013, 406).

This chapter argues that while Ukraine and the EE region are still "defining their place in the international division of academic labour" (Guzzini 2001, 108), their experience can contribute to teaching IR theories in a number of ways. This complicated search for placing Ukraine and EE in the existing knowledge hierarchy stems from a binary dichotomy of IR studies and area studies. The region has been historically considered within Post-Soviet, Post-Communist, or Russia and Eurasia studies (Karczmarska, Ortmann 2021), which localize it in area studies (Politics of East European Area Studies 2016) rather than IR theories, which have been built on Western/great powers' experience (Buzan 2018, 391). In its turn, IR theories have been 'privileged' while area knowledge has limited theoretical value, and "IR theoretics are less reluctant to cite Area Studies (including critical studies and constructivists) than vice versa" (Karczmarska 2020) and "knowledge produced in the periphery has to go through the transatlantic core in order to be recognized globally" (Risse, Wemheuer-Vogelaar, Havemann 2022).

Alejandro and Malksoo explicitly explain the reasons for this hierarchization but are not limited to the late institutionalization and low internationalization of IR in EE that implies late inclusion in IR production; representation of the EE region as "insignificant" both as an agent of world politics and a "locus of knowledge."

(Alejandro 2022, 1001). This representation of the region leads to a situation when Western academic communities speak about others without deep knowledge of the 'insignificant' countries and regions. That leads consequently to misperceptions, misunderstandings and misbeliefs related to regional dynamics. Another reason for a low interest is the concentration of the study of EE within specific sub-fields and associated with the questions and topics of these sub-fields to the exclusion of others — e.g., more represented in international security studies than in IR in general (Malksoo 2021). Though the discussion on the contribution that the EE region can make to IR studies is not new (see Drulak 2009), an ongoing lack of mutual enrichment between IR theories and area studies, separation and hierarchy between them (Karczmarska, Ortmann 2021) stipulates low probability of utilization of empirical material provided by area studies compared to international studies.

Ukraine, being trapped in "epistemological imperialism" (Hendl et al. 2023; Sonevytsky 2022), emerges in the scholarly debates due to the Russian invasion of 2022 and its resilient response, as well as in tributes to Ukrainian scholars affected by the war. To secure the long-standing epistemological value the country and the region present to enriching IR theories development and teaching, we suggest this discussion takes the form of an integrative pluralism (Dunne, 406) and 'pluriversity' that is, in Mbebe's understanding, "a process of knowledge production that is open to epistemic diversity" (Mbembe 2016, 37).

Methodological approach to IR studies syllabi and curricula analysis

Relying on the theoretical approaches discussed above, the research of the IR studies curricula and syllabi pursued a two-fold objective. First, it focused on detecting changes predominantly in MA and PhD curricula of IR studies and syllabi of IR theories related to courses brought by/after the Russian invasion. These changes may be presented by a new course, a module, a topic, or a new reading source related to the lessons learned since the invasion. Special attention was paid to the inclusion of publications of the authors from Ukraine. This author focused on MA/PhD programs on IR studies that included the *Introduction to IR* — the course traditionally delivered to bachelor students. On the one hand, the latter usually utilize traditional mainstream theories while leaving critical theories and postcolonial theories in particular for master's program courses, but, on the other hand, this author tried to check whether the war gave an impetus to re-consider the validity of the mainstream theories through provoking questions for discussion or discussing relevant readings.

Hence, since the research aims to prove the empirical added value of the war-related material for teaching postcolonial studies, another objective set was detecting the utilization of Eastern European (post)colonial experience in teaching critical/postcolonial theories in IR as a part of IR theories or broader IR studies. The latter is considered an appropriate niche where Ukraine's postcolonial experience generalizations, along with neocolonial Russia's politics, could cover those deficiencies that were revealed in the mainstream theories to explain the reasons and nature of the war and actors' behavior. Detections of references to Ukraine or other EE countries in topics, assignments, reading sources, and discussion questions in the syllabi were explored. The analyses of pre-2022 (2015-2022) and after-2022 curricula and syllabi were made. 2015 was selected as the one following Russia's illegal annexation of Crimea and temporary occupation of Eastern Ukrainian territories that could lead to theoretical re-considerations. For this goal, the author analyzed such courses as postcolonial studies, postcolonial theories, postcolonial IR theory, and critical IR theories. Twenty-six universities were selected, with 14 from the US and the UK and 12 from continental Europe, including an analysis of 33 syllabi and 14 curricula (see the tables below).

Complementary to the goals set, the author also paid attention to the utilization of the publications written by scholars from the non-Western world, namely, the Global South, to correlate the trends of decolonizing IR by the inclusion of Global South scholars and decolonizing IR by offering the publications written by scholars from the EE region.

The author's main purpose was to detect changes in the syllabi and/or curricula that occurred after Russia's invasion. Thus, if no Ukraine/war-related content was detected in post-2022 syllabi or the changes directly referred to the war and its consequences, the author skipped searching pre-2022 sources, which apparently could not contain any relevant content. In case regional (not war) related content was present in post-2022 sources, the author searched for pre-2022 sources to understand whether changes were brought by the war or occurred earlier. Taking this into account, the author analyzed ten pre-2022 and 23 post-2022 syllabi.

For this research, the selection of the leading IR/political sciences in Western schools was made based on popular student study portals like 'Topuniversities' (QS World University Rankings 2023), 'Studyportal' (Best IR Schools in the World 2022), 'Shanghai Global Ranking' (Global Ranking of Academic Subjects 2022), which engage 30 to 150 million viewers annually, as well as foreign policy journals and Guardian IR schools rankings (The Best International Relations Schools in the World 2018; Best UK universities for international relations 2024). The rankings of the universities in these ratings are similar. Since IR traditionally stays predominantly in the US-UK field, the majority of universities in the rankings belong to the Anglo-American tradition. However, the European IR tradition, having powerful influence over the continent and globally, studies IR in quite a distinct way and serves as a foundation for selecting universities from Germany, France, Italy, and the Netherlands to secure fair representation of the so-called Western IR tradition and not just the Anglo-American one. Two Canadian universities were also included in the research as IR study and teaching in Canada is very different from the ones in the US (Lipson et al. 2007) as they are attracting an impressive number of students from across the globe.

The main limitation of the research is access to the syllabi and curricula for a consecutive number of years. Many universities lack consistent offers of curricula and syllabi not only for at least five years in a row but sometimes for a current year as well. Sometimes, they upload a brief version of syllabi for open access (without questions/assignments for discussion). Still, the author considers that these limitations did not jeopardize the detection of general trends as all the universities analyzed provided the latest syllabi designed after 2022.

Post-2022 changes in the IR study: results of data analysis and discussion of main findings

The table below represents a visual of the data collected with the respective courses, program level, year of teaching and presence/absence of Ukraine/EE-related topics or assignments, questions for discussion or Ukrainian scholars' publications in the reading list. The last column shows the presence/absence of the respective content on the Global South countries or publications of the scholars representing them in the reading lists.

University	Syllabus	Level of education	Academic year/semester	EE/UA related content/reading	Non-Western countries content/reading
Bristol University	Theories of International Relations	MA	2021-2022 2024-2025	-	-
Freie Universität Berlin	Introduction to International Relations Theories of IR	BA	2021 2024	-	-
Georgetown University	Introduction to International Relations	MA	Summer 2022	-	-
Harvard University	International Relations Field Seminar	MA	Fall 2022	-	+
	Theories of International Relations	MA	2019	-	+

London School of Economics	International Relations: Theories, Concepts and Debates	MA	2022-2023	-	+
	International Relations: Theories, Concepts and Debates	BA	2021-2022	-	+
Martin Luther Universität Halle-Wittenberg	International Relations	BA	2022	+	
McGill University	International Relations as Postcolonial Relations	MA/PhD	Fall 2023	-	+
	Theories of International Relations	MA	Fall 2020	-	+
	Theories of International Relations	MA	Winter2024	-	+
Pennsylvania University	International Relations Theory	PhD	Fall 2023	+	+
Princeton Woodrow Wilson School of Public and Int Affairs	International Politics	MA	2018-2019	-	+
			2023-2024	-	+
SciencesPo	Theories of International Relations	MA	2021-2022	-	-
	Critical Theories of International Relations. The making of the Modern World Order		2021-2022	-	
	Critical Theories of International Relations. The making of the Modern World Order		2023-2024	-	+
Scuola Normale Superiore	Postcolonialism and IR	PhD, MA	2024	+	
University of Bologna	Theories of International Relations (Advanced)	PhD, MA	Fall 2022	+	-
	Theories of International Relations (Advanced)	PhD, MA	Fall 2021	-	-
University of Glasgow	Postcolonial IR theory	PhD	2023-2024	-	+

University of Oslo	Introduction to International Relations	BA	2024-2025	+	+
	International Relations theories	MA	2023-2024	+	+
	International Politics: Key Debates	MA	Autumn 2024	+	+
	International Politics	MA	Summer 2024 Summer 2021	+	+
University of Osnabruck	Introduction to the International Relations	BA	2024	+	
University of London	Postcolonial studies	MA	2023-2024	-	+
University of Toronto	Introduction to International Relations	BA	Summer 2023	-	-
	Postcolonial Debates in International Relations	MA	Winter 2022	-	+
Utrecht University	Postcolonial studies	MA	2024-2025	-	+

CURRICULA/New courses emerged since 2022

Columbia University	Fragmentation of the World: Ukraine and Taiwan as Cases	MA	Fall 2023	+
	Ukraine: Power Politics & Diplomacy	MA	Spring 2024	+
	Ukrainian Foreign Policy: Russia, Europe, and the US		Fall 2022	
	Politics of Identity in Post-Communist Europe		Spring 2024	
Freie Universität Berlin	Russia's attack on Ukraine - geopolitical and geoeconomic perspectives	MA	2023-2024	+
	Russia's War Against Ukraine	MA	2022-2023	+
Humboldt University	Institute for Social Sciences, Faculty of Cultural, Social and Educational Sciences	BA/MA	2023-2024	-
John Hopkins	International Studies	BA/MA	2024	-

University	Course	Level	Year	
Krieger School of Arts and Sciences				
London School of Economics	Eastern Europe: Domestic Regimes and Foreign Policies	PhD, MA	2022-2023	-
SciencesPo	The Russia-Ukraine War: An International Relations Theory Guide Comparative Political Economy: Russia, Ukraine and Belarus	MA	2023-2024	+
	Politics and society in Russia at a time of war in Ukraine		Spring 2024	
	How the war in Ukraine is changing the EU		Spring 2024	
	First Strategic Lessons of the Russian War in Ukraine		Fall 2024	
St. Andrews University	Theoretical Approaches to International Relations — has Postcolonialism	MA	2024-2025	-
University of Amsterdam	International Relations (Political Science)	MA	2024-2025	-
University of Cambridge	International Relations	BA	2022-2023	-
Utrecht University	International Relations (minor)	BA	2024-2025	-

The exploration of the curricula and syllabi has shown a modest splash of interest in Ukraine's experience and its effect on teaching IR — nine out of 33 syllabi and six out of 14 curricula contain changes related to the invasion and/or its consequences. Newly suggested courses belong mainly to elective ones that raise a question about their lifespan. Several universities suggested new courses or topics after the invasion of 2022 for their master's programs in IR. Columbia University offered a course, Politics of Identity in Post-Communist Europe (Columbia University), in 2024, inviting a Ukrainian scholar to teach, focusing on relations between politics and identities in post-communist Eastern, Central and Southern Europe. Free University Berlin suggests a new course,

Russia's attack on Ukraine — geopolitical and geoeconomic perspectives (Freie Universität Berlin 2023-2024), focusing on the examination of the causes and consequences of the invasion from a geopolitical and geoeconomic perspective and the consequences for the EU. The University di Bolognia, within the course Theories of International Relations (Advanced), included the topic "The Ukrainian War" (Universita di Bologna 2022-2023) as one of the perspectives on IR. The University of Halle includes the topic "Genesis and consequences of the war in Ukraine" in the IR course (Martin Luther Universität Halle-Wittenberg 2022).

We could argue with possible reasons for few to no changes in IR curricula/syllabi, namely insufficient time between the invasion start and the research: a lack of publications written by scholars from the region in Anglo-Saxon or Roman languages. However, the first time-related argument is contested by the presence of COVID-19-related courses in the summer semester of 2021 (Georgetown University 2022; Freie Universität Berlin 2021), although this phenomenon has been intervening in social life for a very short period. The second can be contested by a variety of articles that emerged in high-ranking academic journals in 2022-2024 — both *Scopus* and *Web of Science*, written by representatives of the region (Burlyuk, Misliu 2023; Dudko 2022; Golubev 2023; Kurylo 2023 for example). A great example is the syllabus on postcolonialism and IR delivered at Scuola Normale Superiore, where the topic of the invasion is supported by a number of sources, including those written by Ukrainian scholars (Scuola Normale Superiore 2024).

Empirical material generated by Ukraine/Eastern European experience emerges in the curricula and/or syllabi in several capacities. First, as a foundation for reconsideration and theorizing broader topics, which illuminates the limited value that the processes in the region have in theoretical knowledge generation. For example, a number of courses offer the study of the effects the war has on European security and political transformations of the EU (Sciences Po 2024a,b) as well as for nuclear non-proliferation regime perspectives (University of Glasgow 2023-2024a), how the war reflects US decline (Sciences Po). Second, a realist-dominating approach to discussing the war is usually accompanied by Mearsheimer's most famous paper, along with others where the authors try to grasp Russia's politics (e.g., "How we got Putin so wrong," University of Oslo 2024). Third, Ukraine/region-generated material is used more like an exotic case study as to how COVID-19 was represented in previous years or for explaining theories in events, public lectures and roundtables and most probably will be sidelined after the invasion ends.

Along with the ongoing discourses on decolonizing IR and IR differences, African, Asian and Latin American cases are present in the curricula as empirical material for gender studies or modernity, as well as regional security, foreign policy and development studies—e.g., Indian and Latin American politics as separate courses (Freie Universität Berlin 2021; 2024a,b; Columbia University 2023-2024; the University of Glasgow 2023-2024a). Harvard, John Hopkins University, and St. Andrews University have related courses including postcolonial IR studies reflecting on African, Chinese, and Asian IR (Harvard University 2019; University of St. Andrews. 2023-2024; John Hopkins University 2024), Eastern European (post)colonial experience is not suggested. Where postcolonial studies courses are offered as interdisciplinary minors, they have geographic limits—(South) Africa, the Caribbean, India, South America, and Australia and highlight the study of race, gender, class, the violent legacies of slavery along with practices of resistance and national liberation movements which challenged Western thought and brought about global IR transformations (Utrecht University 2024; SciencesPo; SciencesPo 2022-2023; Harvard University 2019; University of Glasgow 2023-2024b). While 19 out of 33 collected syllabi contain references either to topics related to the Global South or offer publications by local scholars, the empirical material on Russia's war against Ukraine—a war of liberation from Russian (neo)colonial practices — publications by Ukrainian scholars still wait to contribute to the courses within the IR/postcolonial realm.

An analysis of the reading lists in a number of syllabi of postcolonial studies/IR reveals the prevalence of traditional works by Fanon, Said, Bhaba, Mbebe, and Spivak, which reflect on Asian and African colonial experience (Freie Universität Berlin 2018-2019, Freie Universität Berlin 2022, University of Toronto 2022, McGill University 2023). Seth's, Dunne's and Tickner's papers on pluralism in IR studies (Seth 2021; Dunne 2013; Tickner 2013) nevertheless are not followed by a proposal for papers reflecting Eastern European experience (Malksoo 2021, 2023; Burlyuk Misliu 2023; Kurylo 2023; Kassymbekova, Chokobaeva 2023; Doyle 2020). Even the fullest reading list on postcolonial IR found in the course syllabus, *Postcolonial IR Theories* at the Glasgow School of Social and Political Sciences, does not suggest any reading on Eastern European practices (University of Glasgow 2023-2024). This shows that postcolonial approaches are still delivered from the angle of Western colonial practices to the affected countries without any reference to Russia's colonial rule patterns and effects.

Considering a broad presence of Russia-related courses, e.g., the foreign and domestic policy of Russia or Russia in world politics at the London School of Economics (2022-2023), Humboldt-Universität zu Berlin (2024), John Hopkins University (2024), and Columbia University (2023-2024), and offer of alternative reasoning of Russia's subaltern imperial behavior (Morozov) in postcolonialism courses (Georgetown University 2020) along with quite a significant scope of inclusion of publications from Global South scholars into the syllabi, the absence of references to Eastern Europe's epistemic contributions raise a question about double marginalization of Ukrainian voices. The syllabi, on the other hand, reflect traditional attention paid to the study of Russia's policies, which is apparently needed to comprehend and predict its behavior (the scope requires additional research, which was not the purpose of the current one). Moreover, on the other hand, they justly include the studies of scholars from the Global South in IR/postcolonial studies.

Ignoring Ukrainian voices in those curricula and syllabi can serve as a manifestation of limited or deprived epistemic agency, which leads to inter-coloniality. The latter exists together with the inter-imperiality when Ukraine-generated knowledge is marginalized by both Western and Russian academia (Hendl 2023; Doyle 2020; Sonevytsky 2022). When we talk about the inter-coloniality of knowledge, we imply silencing the Western academia of Ukrainian (and other regional) voices and ignoring the significance of Ukraine-generated material on the one hand and, on the other, rendering insignificance to Ukrainian (neo)colonial experience in relations with Russia as a colonial empire. Even if new IR courses involving Ukraine-related topics emerge, like *Fragmentation of the World: Ukraine and Taiwan as Cases*, at Columbia University (Columbia University 2023), they ignore Ukraine as a knowledge-productive source, making it voiceless.

Conclusions

The discussion presented shows the need for encouraging ongoing IR decolonizing, deprivation of epistemic hegemony and hierarchy of knowledge production followed by enriching IR theorizing in the teaching process as a means to empower students with diverse epistemological tools. The fact that Russia's invasion brought about few to no changes in the teaching of IR studies in Western academic institutions reflects the ongoing practices of exclusionary hierarchical constructs centered on policies and practices of great powers and institutions. Meanwhile, the role of small/medium powers from within areas, which have not been traditionally considered as colonized in a classical sense, is still marginalized in IR theories, being rather localized into area studies.

The research has shown that Ukraine-generated empirical material and its representation by Ukrainian scholars are either marginalized or included as an object rather than a subject of research, underpinning theoretical constructs or performing as material for the study of more tangible and 'important' issues like European security or non-proliferation regime perspectives. This inference contributes to the discussion on the "power dynamic of epistemic injustice" when Ukrainians are considered "incapable of producing reliable knowledge" (Hendl 2023).

Few post-2022 changes made in the IR studies curricula and syllabi on IR theories and postcolonial studies, which were at the center of the current research, bring several important inferences. First, they show the unreadiness of Western academia to question the explanatory value of mainstream IR theories. Second, the ongoing process of IR decolonization, while outlining moderate progress in a broader inclusiveness of the scholars from the Global South, whose publications are offered in the syllabi on postcolonialism and even IR theories (as part of non-Western IR theories), still lacks recognition of Eastern European postcolonial experience, including the Russia-Ukraine relations. Third, the presence of courses targeting Russia's politics along with Russian scholars in the reading lists without respective Ukrainian components will continue the practices of normalizing Russia's assertiveness and silencing Ukraine's reasons for its behavior and responsive practices.

The presence of these three components brings to the surface the need to search for the tools for overcoming the existing epistemic inter-coloniality embedded in depriving Ukraine of an agency as a knowledge generator and denying its right to possess a respected place in postcolonial studies. Changes that could be expected in the IR/postcolonial studies syllabi and curricula could include the invitation of a larger number of Ukrainian scholars to teach and research, including publications produced by them, especially on Ukraine/EE-related content and on Russia's neocolonial practices. This acceptance and inclusion could relevantly complement the deficiencies of the mainstream IR theories with the toolkit offered by postcolonial approaches.

Substantiation and deeper study of Russian policies and practices in 'near abroad' as (post-/neo-) colonial along with the widely accepted notion of imperial could contribute to IR theory's explanatory potential, placing the EE region in knowledge production. The role of postcolonialism could be a helpful bridge in the better understanding of IR, i.e., power dynamics, colonizer-colonized dichotomy, recognition, identity inferiority, hybridity, and representation. Securing a long-standing reference to the country and region to enrich IR theory development and teaching would correlate with the principles of integrative pluralism (Dunne 2013, 406) and 'pluriversity' that, in Mbebe's understanding, is "a process of knowledge production that is open to epistemic diversity" (Mbebe 2016, 37). Openness to IR studies diversity with integrating EE postcolonial knowledge could help eliminate existing epistemic inequalities and overcome inter-coloniality in Western academia.

Acknowledgment

The author is grateful to the team of editors for the highly relevant initiative, efforts in organizing webinars and academic discussion, and valuable recommendations that contributed to this research, as well as to the team of co-contributors for their cooperation and insightful reflections on the paper. The author is grateful for the support of this research by the European Union, NextGenerationEU. I would also like to thank the reviewers for their valuable feedback and kind advice.

References

Acharya, Amitav. 2014. 'Global International Relations (IR) and Regional Worlds: A New Agenda for International Studies.' *International Studies Quarterly*, Vol. 58, no. 4: 647–659.

Acharya, Amitav and Buzan, Barry. 2017. 'Why is there no non-Western International Relations theory? Ten years on.' *International Relations of the Asia-Pacific*. Vol. 17. no 3: 341-370.

Adamson, Fiona. 2020. 'Pushing the Boundaries: Can We 'Decolonize' Security Studies?' *Journal of Global Security Studies*. Vol. 5, no. 1: 129-135.

Alejandro, Audrey. 2022. 'Do international relations scholars not care about Central and Eastern Europe or do they just take the region for granted?' A conclusion to the special issue. *Journal of International Relations and Development*. Vol.25: 1001–1013.

'Best IR Schools in the World 2022'. https://www.mastersportal.com/articles/2778/best-international-relations-schools-in-the-world-university-rankings-2022.html

'Best UK universities for international relations.' 2024. https://www.theguardian.com/education/ng-interactive/2023/sep/09/best-uk-universities-for-international-relations-league-table

Bhabha, Homi K. 1994. *The Location of Culture*. London and New York: Routledge.

Bouchet, Nicolas. 2015. *Democracy Promotion as US Foreign Policy Bill Clinton and Democratic Enlargement*. London and New York: Routledge.

Burlyuk, Olga and Musliu, Vjosa. 2023. 'The responsibility to remain silent? On the politics of knowledge production, expertise and (self-)reflection in Russia's war against Ukraine'. *Journal of International Relations and Development*. Vol.26: 605–618.

Buzan, Buzan. 2018. 'How and How Not to Develop IR Theory: Lessons from Core and Periphery.' *The Chinese Journal of International Politics*: 391-414.

Chernetsky, Vitaly. 2003. 'Postcolonialism, Russia and Ukraine,' *Ulbandus Review* 7: 32–62.

Columbia University. 2021. 'Theories of International Relations'. *Syllabus*. https://polisci.columbia.edu/sites/default/files/content/pdfs/JackSyllabus%206801%20Theories%20of%20International%20Relations.pdf

Columbia University. 2023. 'Fragmentation of the World: Ukraine and Taiwan as Cases.' https://bulletin.columbia.edu/search/?P=REGN%20U8760

Columbia University. 2023-2024. *Political Science. 2023-2024 Year at a glance*. https://polisci.columbia.edu/content/2023-24-year-glance

Columbia University. 2024. 'Politics of Identity in Post-Communist Europe.' *Syllabus*. https://bulletin.columbia.edu/search/?P=REGN%20U6520

Copeland, Dale C. 1996. 'Economic Interdependence and War: A Theory of Trade Expectations' *International Security.* Vol.20. no.4: 5-41.

Davis, A., Thakur, V. and Vale, P. 2020. *The Imperial Discipline: Race and the Founding of International Relations.* London: Pluto Press.

Davis, Norman. 2022. 'Decolonizing Eastern European Studies: Interview with Professor Norman Davies,' Cambridge University Ukrainian Society, 16 June, available at https://www.facebook.com/CUUA soc/videos/decolonizing-eastern-european-studies-interview-with-professor-norman-davies/1560014551062883/

Donovan, Victoria. 2023. 'Against academic 'resourcification': collaboration as delinking from extractivist 'area studies' paradigms,' *Canadian Slavonic Papers.* Vol.65. no.2: 163-173.

Doyle, Laura. 2020. *Inter imperiality: Vying empires, gendered labor, and the literary arts of alliance.* Duke University Press.

Drulak, Petr. 2009. 'Going Native? The Discipline of IR in Central and Eastern Europe'. *Przeglad Europejski,* Vol.1. No. 27: 10-14.

Dudko, Oksana. 2022. 'A conceptual limbo of genocide: Russian rhetoric, mass atrocities in Ukraine, and the current definition's limits', *Canadian Slavonic Papers,* Vol.64. no.2-3: 133-145.

Dunne, T., Hansen, L., Wight, C. 2013. 'The end of International Relations theory?' *European Journal of International Relations.* Vol.19, no.3.

Dutkiewicz, Jan and Smolenski, Jan. 2023. 'Epistemic superimposition: the war in Ukraine and the poverty of expertise in international relations theory.' *Journal of International Relations and Development.* Vol. 26: 619-631.

Fanon, Frantz. 1963. *The Wretched of the Earth,* New York: Grove Press.

'Foreign Policy Concept of the Russian Federation'. 2000. Approved by the President of the Russian Federation 28 June 2000, available at https://docs.cntd.ru/document/901764263

Freie Universität Berlin. 2018-2019. 'Introduction into Postcolonial Theory and Critique'. https://www.polsoz.fu-berlin.de/polwiss/forschu ng/international/frieden/lehre/2018_19ws/15364_S/index.html

Freie Universität Berlin. 2021. 'Otto Suhr Institute for Political Science.' https://archiv.vv.fu-berlin.de/ss21/en/module/0257b_MA120/

Freie Universität Berlin. 2022. 'Lektürekurs: Frantz Fanon und die postkoloniale Theorie'. https://www.fu-berlin.de/vv/de/lv/731190?m= 183688&p=183643&pc=74963&sm=682080

Freie Universität Berlin. 2023-2024. 'Russlands Angriff auf die Ukraine— geopolitische und geoökonomische Perspektiven'. https://www.fu-berlin.de/vv/en/lv/809069?m=409798&pc=575029&sm=754328

Freie Universität Berlin. 2024a. 'Global IR: Kritische Perspektiven zu 'Internationalen Beziehungen' in Asien.' https://www.fu-berlin.de/vv/en/lv/882065?m=409818&pc=575029&sm=814672&id=882065

Freie Universität Berlin. 2024b. 'Masterstudiengang Internationale Beziehungen.' https://www.fu-berlin.de/vv/de/modul?id=575029&sm=814672

Gallien, Claire. 2020. 'A Decolonial Turn in the Humanities.' *Journal of Comparative Poetics*, vol.40: 28-58.

Gat, Azar. 2005. 'The Democratic Peace Theory Reframed: The Impact of Modernity,' *World Politics*. Vol. 58. No.1: 73–100.

Georgetown University. 2020. 'Postcolonialism'. *Syllabus.* available at https://giwps.georgetown.edu/wp-content/uploads/2020/10/Postcolonialism.pdf

Georgetown University. 2022. 'Introduction to International Relations.' *Syllabus.* https://static.scs.georgetown.edu/upload/files/syllabi/term_202220/course_GOVT-060/section_21/GOVT060-21.pdf

'Global Ranking of Academic Subjects'. *Political Sciences* 2022. https://www.shanghairanking.com/rankings/gras/2022/RS0504

Golubev, Alexey. 2023. 'No natural colonization: the early Soviet school of historical anti-colonialism.' *Canadian Slavonic Papers*. Vol.65. no.2: 190-204.

Guzzini, S. 2001. 'The significance and roles of teaching theory in international relations.' *Journal of International Relations and Development*. Vol.4: 98-117.

Hagström, Linus. 2021. 'Great Power Narcissism and Ontological (In)Security: The Narrative Mediation of Greatness and Weakness in International Politics.' *International Studies Quarterly*. Vol. 65. No. 2: 331-342.

Harvard University. 2019. 'Theories of International Relations'. *Syllabus.* https://scholar.harvard.edu/files/brianpalmiter/files/POLSCI380.syllabus.spring_2019.pdf

Hassan, S. and Sajjad, F. 2022. 'The Decolonial Turn: New Challenges to International Relations Traditions.' *Journal of Contemporary Studies*. Vol. 11. No.2: 23–41.

Hendl, Tereza, Burlyuk, Olga, O'Sullivan Mila, Arystanbek, Aizada. 2023. '(En)Countering epistemic imperialism: A critique of "Westsplaining" and coloniality in dominant debates on Russia's invasion of Ukraine.' *Contemporary Security Policy*. Vol.45. No.2: 171-209.

Hoffman, S. 1977. 'An American Social Science: International Relations.' *Daedalus*. vol.106. no.3: 41-60.

Humboldt-Universität zu Berlin. 2024. 'Heilige Rus und 'Russische Welt'. https://agnes.hu-berlin.de/lupo/rds?state=verpublish&status=init&vmfile=no&publishid=214755&moduleCall=webInfo&publishConfFile=webInfo&publishSubDir=veranstaltung

Hutchings, K. 2023. 'Doing epistemic justice in International Relations: women and the history of international thought.' *European Journal of International Relations*. Vol. 29, no. 4.

John Hopkins University. 2024. Program in International Studies. https://krieger.jhu.edu/internationalstudies/undergraduate/courses/course-schedule/

Kaczmarska, K. 2020. *Making Global Knowledge in Local Contexts: The Politics of International Relations and Policy Advice in Russia.* London, New York: Routledge.

Kaczmarska, Katarzyna and Ortmann, Stefanie. 2021. 'IR theory and Area Studies: a plea for displaced knowledge about international politics.' *Journal of International Relations and Development*. Vol.24: 820-847.

Kassymbekova, Botakoz. 2022. 'Empires and Nation-States: the Russian-Ukrainian War and Decolonizing of Eastern European Studies,' *Deutsch-Ukrainische Historische Kommission*, 17 November, available at https://www.youtube.com/watch?v=qL26qQXwjS0 (12 February, 2024).

Kassymbekova, Botakoz, Chokobaeva, Aminat. (2023). 'Expropriation, assimilation, elimination: Understanding Soviet Settler Colonialism.' *South/South Dialogues*. https://www.southsouthmovement.org/dialogues/expropriation-assimilation-elimination-understanding-soviet-settler-colonialism/.

Kazharski, Aliaksei. 2022. 'Explaining the 'Westsplainers': Can a Western Scholar be an Authority on Central and Eastern Europe?', *Forum for Ukrainian Studies*, 19 July, available at https://ukrainian-studies.ca/2022/07/19/explaining-the-westsplainers-can-a-western-scholar-be-an-authority-on-central-and-eastern-europe/

Khylko, Olena. 2017. 'Security Options for Eastern Europe,' *Wschód Europy. Studia Humanistyczno-Społeczne*. Vol. 3. No.2: 67-80.

Koplatadze, Tamar. 2019. 'Theorising Russian postcolonial studies,' *Postcolonial Studies*. Vol. 22. No.4: 469-489.

Küçük, Mine Nur. 2022. 'Postcolonial Approaches in International Relations' in M. Kürşad Özekin and Engin Sune, eds., *Critical Approaches to International Relations: Philosophical Foundations and Current Debates*, 157-174, Leiden: Brill.

Kurylo, Bohdana. 2023. 'The Ukrainian subject, hierarchies of knowledge production and the everyday: An autoethnographic narrative,' *Journal of International Relations and Development*, Vol.26: 685-697.

Lipson, Michael, Maliniak, Daniel, Oakes, Amy, Peterson, Susan, Tierney, Michael J. 2007. 'Divided Discipline? Comparing Views of US and Canadian IR Scholars', *International Journal*, Vol. 62, No. 2: 327-343.

London School of Economics. 2022-2023. 'International Relations Courses.' Master Programme. https://info.lse.ac.uk/current-students/services/assets/documents/Controlled-access-courses-22-23-PDF.pdf

Makarychev, Andrey and Nizhnikau, Ryhor. 2023. 'Normalize and rationalize: Intellectuals of statecraft and Russia's war in Ukraine,' *Journal of International Relations and Development*. Vol.26: 632-642.

Mälksoo, M. 2021. 'Captive minds: the function and agency of Eastern Europe in International Security Studies.' *Journal of International Relations and Development*. Vol.24: 866-889.

Mälksoo, Maria. 2023. 'The Postcolonial Moment in Russia's War Against Ukraine,' *Journal of Genocide Research*. Vol.25. no.3-4: 471-481.

Manners, Ian. 2024. 'Arrival of Normative Power in Planetary Politics,' *Journal of Common Market Studies*. Vol.62. no.3: 825-844.

Martin Luther Universität Halle-Wittenberg. 2022. 'Vorlesung: BA Basismodul Einführung in die Internationalen Beziehungen – (Vorlesung)'. https://studip.uni-halle.de/dispatch.php/course/details/?sem_id=078c8f5e3d9ee2801b3e78ed14ac93d4&send_from_search=1&send_from_search_page=https%3A%2F%2Fstudip.uni-halle.de%3A443%2Fdispatch.php%3Fkeep_result_set%3D1&set_language=de_DE

Mbembe, Achille. 2016. 'Decolonizing the university: New directions.' *Arts and Humanities in Higher Education*. vol.15. no.1: 29-45.

McGill University. 2023. 'International Relations As Postcolonial Relation'. Syllabus. https://www.mcgill.ca/politicalscience/files/politicalscience/poli676_syllabus_f23_final.pdf

Mearsheimer, John J. 2014. 'Why the Ukraine Crisis Is the West's Fault. The Liberal Delusions That Provoked Putin,' *Foreign Affairs*. Vol. 93. No.5: 77-89.

Moore, David Chioni. 2001. 'Is the Post- in Postcolonial the Post- in Post-Soviet? Toward a Global Postcolonial Critique', *PMLA*. Vol. 116. No.1: 111-128.

Morozov, Viatcheslav. 2015. *Russia's Postcolonial Identity: A Subaltern Empire in a Eurocentric World*, London: Palgrave Macmillan.

Müller, Martin. 2020. 'In Search of the Global East: Thinking between North and South.' *Geopolitics*. Vol.25. no.3: 735-755.

Nye, Joseph S. Jr. 2022a. 'Eight Lessons from the Ukraine War,' *Project Syndicate*, 15 June, available at https://www.project-syndicate.org/commentary/russia-war-in-ukraine-eight-lessons-by-joseph-s-nye-2022-06

Nye, Joseph S. Jr. 2022b. 'What Caused the Ukraine War?', *Project Syndicate*, 04 October, available at https://www.project-syndicate.org/commentary/what-caused-russia-ukraine-war-by-joseph-s-nye-2022-10

O'Sullivan, Míla and Krulišová, Kateřina. 2023. 'Central European subalterns speak security (too): Towards a truly post-Western feminist security studies,' *Journal of International Relations and Development*. Vol. 26: 660–674.

Pavlyshyn, Marko. 1993. 'Ukrainian Literature and the Erotics of Postcolonialism: Some Modest Propositions,' *Harvard Ukrainian Studies*, Vol.17. no.1/2: 110–126.

Risse, Thomas, Wemheuer-Vogelaar, Wiebke, Havemann Frank (2022). 'IR Theory and the Core–Periphery Structure of Global IR: Lessons from Citation Analysis.' *International Studies Review*, Vol.24, no. 3.

Robles, Alfredo C. Jr. 1993. 'How 'International' Are International Relations Syllabi?' *Political Science and Politics*, Vol.26, no.3: 526-528.

'QS World University Rankings by Subject 2023: Politics'. https://www.topuniversities.com/university-subject-rankings/politics

Said, Edward W. 1979. *Orientalism*. New York: Vintage Books.

Schultz, Kenneth. 2013. 'Domestic Politics and International Relations' In *Handbook of International Relations*, Ed. by Walter Carlsnaes, Thomas Risse, Beth A. Simmons. London: SAGE Publications.

Sciences Po. 2022-2023. 'Critical Theories of International Relations. The making of the Modern World Order.' https://syllabus.sciencespo.fr/cours/202220/223147.html

Sciences Po. 2024a. 'Comment la guerre d'Ukraine change l'UE.' Master Programme. https://syllabus.sciencespo.fr/fr/?mapping/189362

Sciences Po. 2024b. 'First Strategic Lessons of the Russian War in Ukraine.' Master Programme in International Security. https://syllabus.sciencespo.fr/fr/?mapping/189375

Sciences Po. 'The Russia-Ukraine War. An International Relations Theory Guide'. *Syllabus*. https://www.sciencespobordeaux.fr/fr/formation/diplome-d-institut-d-etudes-politiques/deuxieme-cycle-parcours-de-masters-cycle2/bordeaux-international-relations-degree-bird-ICOS4UK2/quatrieme-annee-bird-K49N69MV/the-russia-ukraine-war-an-international-relations-theory-guide-LAQNFF1O.html

Scuola Normale Superiore. 2024. 'Postcolonialism and International Relations.' *Syllabus*. https://www.sns.it/en/corsoinsegnamento/postcolonialism-and-international-relations

Seth, Sanjay 2021. 'International relations: plural or postcolonial?' *International Politics Reviews*.

Spivak, Gayatri Chakravorty, Condee, Nancy, Ram, Harsha and Chernetsky, Vitaly. 2006. 'Are We Postcolonial? Post-Soviet Space', *PMLA*. Vol. 121. No.3: 828-836.

Smith, S. 1995. 'The Self-Images of a Discipline. International Relations Theory Today'. Edited by Booth, K. and Smith, S. Oxford: Polity Press: 1-37.

Snyder, Timothy. 2022. 'The War in Ukraine is a Colonial War,' *The New Yorker*, 28 April, available at https://www.newyorker.com/news/essay/the-war-in-ukraine-is-a-colonial-war

Sonevytsky, Maria. 2022. 'What Is Ukraine? Notes On Epistemic Imperialism', *Topos*. Vol. 2: 21-30.

Szeptycki, Andrzej. 2011. 'Ukraine as A Postcolonial State?', *The Polish Quarterly of International Affairs*. Vol.20. no.1: 5-29.

'The Best International Relations Schools in the World'. 2018. https://foreignpolicy.com/2018/02/20/top-fifty-schools-international-relations-foreign-policy/

'The Politics of East European Area Studies.' 2016. Edited by Gareth Dale, Katalin Miklossy, Dieter Segert. Routledge.

Tlostanova, M., Mignolo W. 2012. 'Learning to Unlearn: Decolonial Reflections From Eurasia and the Americas'. Oxford State University Press. 281p.

Tickner, Arlene. 2013. 'Core, Periphery and (Neo)Imperialist International Relations.' *European Journal of International Relations*. Vol. 19. No. 3: 627-646.

Todorova, Maria. 1997. *Imagining the Balkans*. Oxford, Oxford University Press: 272.

Tolz, Vera and Hutchings, Stephen. 2023. 'Truth with a Z: disinformation, war in Ukraine, and Russia's contradictory discourse of imperial identity,' *Post-Soviet Affairs*. Vol.39. no.5: 347-365.

Trenin, Dmitriy. 2013. 'The Fourth Vector of Vladimir Putin,' *Russia in Global Politics*. 30 May, available at https://globalaffairs.ru/articles/chetvertyj-vektor-vladimira-putina/

Tucker, K. 2018. 'Unraveling Coloniality in International Relations: Knowledge, Relationality, and Strategies for Engagement'. *International Political Sociology*. Vol. 12. No.3: 215-232.

Universität Bremen. 'Ukraine. 'Zur Erklärung eines Angriffskrieges.' https://www.uni-bremen.de/suchen?q=Kritische+Theorie+syllabus

Universita di Bologna. 2022-2023. 'Theories Of International Relations (Advanced).' *Syllabus.* https://www.unibo.it/en/teaching/course-unit-catalogue/course-unit/2022/484996

University of Glasgow. 2023-2024a. 'Politics 1B: Introduction to International Relations.' https://rl.talis.com/3/glasgow/lists/CFA9C287-3497-A3B9-C6D2-8FF867164F19.html?lang=en-GB

University of Glasgow. 2023-2024b. 'Post-colonial IR theory. Reading list.' https://rl.talis.com/3/glasgow/lists/92FDFD55-30D5-BBF2-E092-125C9B1B7767.html?lang=en

University of St. Andrews. 2023-2024. 'Theoretical Approaches to International Relations.' https://www.st-andrews.ac.uk/subjects/modules/catalogue/?code=IR2005&academic_year=2023%2F4

University of Toronto. 2022. 'Postcolonial Debates in IR.' https://politics.utoronto.ca/wp-content/uploads/syllabus/2122_pol486h1s_l0101.pdf

Utrecht University. 2024. Postcolonial Studies. https://students.uu.nl/en/academics/minors/postcolonial-studies

Wæver, O., Tickner, A. 2009. 'Geocultural epistemologies. International Relations Scholarship Around the World.' Edited by Wæver, O., Tickner, A. Routledge.

Walt, Stephen M. 2022. 'Liberal Illusions Caused the Ukraine Crisis,' *Foreign Policy*, 19 January, available at https://foreignpolicy.com/2022/01/19/ukraine-russia-nato-crisis-liberal-illusions/ (12 February, 2024).

Waltz, K. 1986. 'A Response to My Critics,' in Robert O. Keohane, ed., *Neorealism and its Critics.* New York: Columbia University Press, 1986

Wendt, Alexander. 1992. 'Anarchy is what States Make of it: The Social Construction of Power Politics.' *International Organization* vol. 46. No. 2: 391–425.

Wilkens, Jan. 2017. 'Postcolonialism in International Relations.' *Oxford Research Encyclopedia of International Studies, International Relations Association and Oxford University Press*, 20 November, available at https://doi.org/10.1093/acrefore/9780190846626.013.101

Wolff, Larry. 1994. *Inventing Eastern Europe. The Map of Civilization on the Mind of the Enlightenment.* Stanford University Press: 436.

Zondi, S. 2016. 'A decolonial turn in diplomatic theory: unmasking epistemic injustice.' *Journal of Contemporary History.* vol.41. no. 1.

Teaching International Political Economy in Times of War

Thomas Fetzer

For scholars of IPE based in Europe, Russia's aggression against Ukraine and the ensuing largest military conflict on the continent since World War II has posed a fundamental challenge not only to their field of research but also to their teaching practices. This is so primarily because IPE as a discipline, a few exceptions aside (see, e.g., Strange, 1994), has had little to say about how its field of studies relates to questions of peace, war, and security during the last decades. This relative neglect is discernible, for example, in mainstream IPE textbooks, some of which have featured a chapter on global security without many linkages to the analysis of the global economy (e.g., Balaam and Dillman, 2019), while others hastily added a few snippets on the Russo-Ukrainian war and 'weaponized interdependence' only after the invasion in 2022 (e.g., Oatley, 2022). The same picture prevails in the more specialized literature, as evidenced in flagship journals such as the *Review of International Political Economy* (RIPE). In a special issue celebrating RIPE's 30th anniversary, the editors provided a comprehensive list of the core themes covered in the journal's history, ranging from trade, global value chains, international money and finance to tax governance, labor, health and environment, as well as the IPE of development—but they made no mention of war, peace and security (Bair et al. 2023).

Perhaps the starkest illustration of IPE's 'sanitization' of the discipline from security issues is the recently proliferating scholarship on the interwar crisis of global capitalism, which is informed by a quest to draw analogies and learn historical lessons to address the contemporary globalization predicament. Predominantly steeped into a Polanyian approach to the history of capitalism as a 'double movement' between the disembedding and re-embedding of global markets from and into bounded social and territorial compacts, this scholarship addresses the interwar crisis — in retrospective reading from the present — almost exclusively as a crisis of social and economic cohesion (see, e.g., Fraser 2014; Burawoy 2015). However, the interconnection between the crisis of economic globalization and the broader crisis of the interwar international order has been a crucial preoccupation of key contemporary thinkers — from John Maynard Keynes to the incipient neoliberal circles (see, e.g., Mulder 2022).

Against the backdrop of this general neglect of issues of security in the discipline, the question of how to teach IPE in the current times of war poses a major challenge, and the remainder of this chapter can only provide a few preliminary reflections to this end.[1] It does so in two steps. First, in a perspective drawing from the sociology of knowledge production in IR (see Burlyuk et al., 2023), it seeks to demonstrate the pedagogical usefulness of systematic engagement with the shortcomings of several mainstream IPE approaches in making sense of the interrelation between the international economic and security orders, including reflections on how these shortcomings have contributed to misperceptions of the Russo-Ukrainian conflict prior and subsequent to the start of Russia's full-scale invasion in February 2022. This will be explored in relation to liberal and neo-Marxist IPE approaches. In the second part, the article addresses the question of how best to engage with the conceptual tools warranted to ground classroom discussions of IPE in times of war, primarily through the exploration of the concept of 'weaponized interdependence.' The final section concludes.

---

1 These reflections are based on experiences of teaching IPE courses since the outbreak of Russia's full-scale invasion against Ukraine, at Central European University's International Relations department in 2022 and 2023.

IPE knowledge production and the interrelation between economic and security orders

A growing and interdisciplinary body of recent work has highlighted how the Russo-Ukrainian war has exposed shortcomings in academic knowledge production in IR, particularly in relation to the East European region, where scholars are at the forefront of lively debates about how to overcome the implicit epistemological, ontological and normative biases of extant Western-dominated writing on the region (see Burlyuk et al., 2023). Against this backdrop, an emphasis on the politics of knowledge production is a crucial and pedagogically essential element of teaching IPE in times of war. The Russo-Ukrainian war can be extensively drawn upon to convey to students how assumptions of various disciplinary paradigms, coupled with broader normative beliefs, have translated into specific approaches toward the economy-security nexus prior to and after the 2022 invasion and how this has politically mattered in shaping public debates and policies. In the following, I illustrate this perspective through selected examples of work drawn from the liberal and neo-Marxist IPE paradigms.

(Neo)liberal approaches

From a classroom perspective, the Russo-Ukrainian war can be used in multiple ways to highlight key assumptions and policy implications of (neo)liberal IPE approaches, but energy policy is perhaps the most straightforward option. It is easy to highlight the significance of energy policy for the conflict prior to and during the war, while linkages to liberal IPE paradigms can be demonstrated in a variety of ways.

A good starting point for class discussion is to ask students to grapple with the magnitude of Europe's dependence on Russian oil and gas prior to February 2022 and, using statistics and/or video material of speeches of key decision-makers, to highlight the implications of this dependence in terms of the limitations placed on EU sanctions against Russia to avoid sudden supply shortages, as well as in terms of the massive contribution European energy payments have been making to finance Russia's war. Moreover, students can be encouraged to think about the costly efforts to diversify European oil and gas supplies away from Russia since 2022, both in relation to domestic economic difficulties and to the turmoil caused by global energy markets (see Siddi, 2022).

To link these patterns of European energy policy to liberal IPE, a class discussion can then proceed in different ways. One possibility is to take a closer look at the origins of Europe-Russia energy relations during the Cold War, with particular attention to the FRG's new *Ostpolitik* of the 1970s, which coincided with Soviet-German agreements to build a gas pipeline network connecting West Germany with newly discovered Siberian gas fields. While at the time predominantly seen through the lens of East-West security co-operation and détente, *Ostpolitik* bore a strong imprint of liberal IPE approaches in terms of the conceptualization of how domains of 'low politics' such as energy cooperation (or social and cultural exchange) might, over time, entail the peaceful transformation of 'high politics' antagonisms—reminiscent of liberal debates on the nexus between peace and economic cooperation since Kant's "perpetual peace" (see Russett et al. 1998). This discussion can be further deepened through a linkage with post-Cold War debates on the liberal international order, in particular with regard to the widespread liberal expectations that previously Western institutions such as the World Trade Organisation (WTO) could be turned into vehicles to spread liberal economic principles and practices across the globe (see Ikenberry 2018).

Another option is to focus more directly on the development of the EU's energy policy since the 1990s. Here, following a familiarization with the institutional basics of the European Single Market in the energy sector, students can be invited to engage with case studies of EU-Russia energy relations, for example, particular pipeline projects (North Stream) or key pieces of legislation such as the 2019 EU gas directive. Exploring in depth the EU's regulatory policies toward Gazprom, with its emphasis on non-discrimination and competition law rules, can provide particularly compelling evidence of the impact of liberal IPE paradigms (see Goldthau and Sitter 2015). In terms of the broader political framing of EU energy policy, it is useful to highlight, on the one hand, the frequent emphasis on how deep economic integration is assumed to shape Russia's opportunity costs in the direction of a 'trading' (rather than an 'invading') state (Rosecrance 1986), while also, on the other hand, paying attention to the EU's self-identification as a liberal international actor that, for the sake of its credible commitment to a liberal world order, ought to refrain from open mercantilist policies (see Goldthau and Sitter 2015).

As highlighted earlier, a pedagogical focus on knowledge production requires that discussion should not be limited to the analysis of policies and institutions but should place strong emphasis on the contested nature of knowledge production. Again, the field of EU energy policy lends itself very well to this task, as contestation of core (neo)liberal assumptions of the policy, voiced predominantly by scholars and policy experts from Central and Eastern Europe, goes back to the mid-2000s. Anita Orban's (2008) analysis of Russia's geopolitical approach to European energy relations provides a compelling early case of such CEE critiques; other suitable examples include the work of Ukrainian and Polish scholars like Olena Viter (2006) and Jakub Godzimirski (2019). Engagement with these works helps students understand how liberal notions of the relationship between energy cooperation and peace, while acquiring intellectual hegemony in the post-Cold War period, have been questioned from the Eastern 'periphery' of the EU for a long time. In turn, this can then be related to post-2022 controversies about 'what went wrong' in Europe's energy policy, where CEE experts' earlier positions have frequently been vindicated.[2]

---

2   See for example: https://www.brookings.edu/articles/how-did-germany-fare-without-russian-gas/

To highlight the usefulness of a knowledge production approach to teaching IPE in times of war, class discussion can conclude on a forward-looking note that points to the persistent importance of (neo)liberal IPE to address the future of European energy policy. On the one hand, while very few scholars and policy experts still endorse notions of energy policy as 'low politics,' the knowledge production battles about EU energy policy are now being conducted in terms of concepts of resilience and the question of how geopolitics relates to the renewable energy transition (see Vakulchuk et al. 2020). On the other hand, it is worth pointing out that energy is just one among other policy challenges facing liberal democracies in the future in terms of determining the parameters of engagement with systemic rivals and competitors—beyond the case of Russia. The 'take-away' for students should be that (neo)liberal IPE will still be a major point of reference in future debates about how liberal democracies are to adjust their strategies and policies in a new 'geoeconomic' international order (Roberts et al. 2019).

Neo-Marxist approaches

Compared to the rather straightforward association of the Russo-Ukrainian war with (neo)liberal IPE, the relevance of neo-Marxist IPE approaches may seem rather questionable. However, this can be addressed through student engagement with key narratives of anti-war protests and opposition to Western military support for Ukraine, in which, on the left side of the political spectrum, arguments of the nexus between global capitalism and Western imperialism often loom large. In other words, the relevance of neo-Marxist IPE lies less in its direct impact on policies than in the influence on segments of public opinion in Western Europe and North America. To engage student audiences with neo-Marxist IPE knowledge production in more detail, it is advisable to focus on well-known scholars whose work is widely recognized while they also appear in broader public debates. This is illustrated here through the examples of David Harvey and Radhika Desai.

Harvey, a bestselling neo-Marxist economic geographer and anthropologist, is perhaps best known to a broader audience through his work on new imperialism, in which he argues that the United States, the global hegemon of neoliberal capitalism, faces structural economic decline driven by the rise of systemic competitors like China, which is accompanied by the acceleration of domestic social and political tensions, and which entails a drift toward direct political and military expansionism to secure resources and markets for the future (Harvey 2005). Students can directly engage with these arguments through Harvey's brief 2022 text "Remarks on Recent Events in the Ukraine: A Provisional Statement" and a follow-up video podcast in which he places the Russo-Ukrainian war into his wider framework of interpretation. In this view, we are dealing with a "capitalist war" through which a challenged US hegemon seeks to reassert its dominance while getting rid of domestic surplus capital.[3] It is particularly instructive to focus class discussion on questions of agency here, which, for Harvey, rests almost exclusively with the West or, indeed, the United States. Russia's role is reduced to having been victimized by the Western "shock therapy" of the 1990s, while Ukraine, fighting an American proxy war, faces total neo-liberalization at the hands of Western capital.

Radhika Desai, a key member of the Geopolitical Economy Research Centre based at the University of Manitoba (Canada), reaches similar conclusions from slightly different theoretical assumptions. Drawing on world-systems analysis and state capitalism literature, Desai likens global capitalism to neocolonial exploitation of world peripheries, whose resistance finds expression in state-directed development strategies that, in turn, increasingly threaten to overturn Western hegemony (Desai 2013). Within this

---

3   https://www.youtube.com/watch?v=NEZP_RzT2Dk [accessed 22 April 2024].

pattern, Desai portrays Russia as a challenger to Western neoimperialism and Ukraine as a key battlefield in Russia's resistance against the West's project to undermine state-directed alternative economic development models; Russia itself is explicitly referred to as a non-imperialist power. Even following Russia's invasion in 2022, Desai has doubled down on her arguments, and her highly controversial public appearance with Putin at the Valdai Club in October 2023 can serve as a useful starting point for a class discussion to explore how neo-Marxist IPE paradigms can shape attitudes toward the Russo-Ukrainian war among segments of academia and public opinion in Western Europe and North America.[4]

To deepen this discussion, as in the case of (neo)liberal IPE, systematic attention needs then to be paid to the contested nature of knowledge production, addressing the controversies triggered by Harvey's and Desai's writings on the Russo-Ukrainian war, not least within left-leaning academic circles themselves. Depending on the author's choice, this can focus on slightly different issues: For the Harvey debate, the most straightforward approach would be the engagement with 'Westsplaining' critiques (see Hendl et al., 2023) targeting Harvey's above-mentioned exclusive emphasis on the role of the United States, while denying any meaningful agency to either Russia or Ukraine (see, e.g., Hall 2022). Regarding Desai, the debate can more specifically focus on engagement with her explicit denial of Russian imperialism, which has been contested even by scholars operating within an overall Marxist approach to imperialism (see Gowans 2023). Again, as with (neo)liberal IPE, this can be connected to a broader reflection on the contestation of spatial hierarchies of knowledge production through the foregrounding of the prominence of intellectuals from Central and Eastern Europe in these debates.

A pedagogically compelling conclusion to such a discussion, in analogy to the earlier elaborated engagement with (neo)liberal

---

4   https://www.cbc.ca/news/canada/manitoba/radhika-desai-valdai-russia-ukraine-1.6995250

IPE, could address the broader significance of neo-Marxist IPE for contemporary academic and policy debates beyond the case of the Russo-Ukrainian war. One key issue in this regard would be the exploration of the ways in which neo-Marxist IPE paradigms shape broader knowledge production patterns of global economic relations through their predominant focus on the exploitation of the Global South by the Global North, in particular with regard to legacies of European colonialism. Contextualizing and problematizing these patterns by bringing in recent debates on the neglect of the Global East (see Müller 2020) can help students understand at once the continued salience of neo-Marxist IPE approaches, as well as the contested nature of all IPE knowledge production.

Conceptual tools to ground IPE in times of war: The example of 'weaponized interdependence'

Beyond engaging with important questions of the politics of knowledge production, the perhaps most crucial challenge to address in teaching IPE in times of war is the question of how to conceptually ground classroom discussions in ways that make it easy to 'bring' the Russo-Ukrainian war to the classroom, while, at the same time, allowing for wider analytical contextualization in extant scholarship and ongoing debates about the changing nature of the international economic order. Such conceptual grounding is particularly important in light of the above-mentioned general paucity of IPE engagement with questions of war and security.

While there is, of course, no one best way to address this challenge, I suggest that the concept of 'weaponized interdependence' (WI) can provide significant support in delivering these tasks of structuring classroom discussions. First proposed by Farrell and Newman (2019), the core idea of this concept is to rethink mainstream assumptions on international economic interdependence mostly derived from liberal IR theory in the wake of Kant's *Perpetual Peace*, namely that economic interdependence raises states' opportunity costs in such a way that they face prohibitive penalties for disrupting interdependence, thus creating a virtuous circle of interstate cooperation and peace (see Rosecrance 1986). WI analytically foregrounds the opposite dynamic whereby (groups of) states, if they are in a position of control over particular economic nodes and networks, can make strategic use of this interdependence for their own purposes — "to discover and exploit vulnerabilities, compel policy change, and deter unwanted action" (Farrell and Newman 2019: 45). This happens through two main channels conceptualized as 'panopticon' and 'chokepoint' effects; in the former, controlling states use their network position to extract informational advantages vis-à-vis adversaries, whereas in the latter, they can cut adversaries off from networks altogether (Farrell and Newman 2019: 46).

Despite its very recent origin, the WI concept has already gained significant traction in the literature as scholars seek to apply and develop it in a range of geographical and sectoral domains (see, e.g., Chang and Yang 2020; Gjesvik 2023). In parallel, a vivid epistemological debate on the analytical limits and possible abuse of the concept has also emerged, which enhances the potential of WI to inform classroom debate contexts (see Drezner et al. 2021). In the following, these advantages are further explored with particular reference to the potential to bring the Russo-Ukrainian war 'into the classroom' and to provide openings into broader debates about international economic order.

'Weaponized interdependence' and classroom discussions on the Russo-Ukrainian war

The WI concept is very well suited to connect abstract reflection on the economy-security nexus with the concrete empirical reality of the Russo-Ukrainian war. The ongoing war not only illustrates the functioning of key mechanisms of WI, here, in particular, the 'chokepoint effect,' but can also serve to discuss limitations of applicability, not least regarding assumptions of hierarchical control of economic networks, as well as considerations addressing potential longer-term negative fallout of the strategic use of WI.

On the one hand, this dynamic can be brought into the classroom through the analysis of Russia's use of the 'energy chokehold,' particularly in the gas sector with its pipeline infrastructure and long-term producer-buyer relations (see Grigas 2017). The basic functioning of 'chokepoint effects' can be easily highlighted through the reconstruction of the build-up of Russian dominance in European gas markets since the 1990s (see Orban 2008) and of the subsequent leveraging of this dominance. For the latter, a focused case analysis of Russian-Ukrainian gas conflicts since the 2004 Orange Revolution is particularly well suited, highlighting multiple occasions of gas supply stoppages, as well as stoppage threats as a recurring coercive Russian bargaining strategy, not least against the backdrop of Ukraine's importance as a transit country for Russian gas deliveries to Central and Western Europe.

This analysis of the pre-2022 conflict can then be contrasted with developments following Russia's invasion, which point to a much more ambiguous picture of the salience of WI. To grasp these dynamics, students can be encouraged to delve into the details of Russian supply disruption efforts in the spring and summer of 2022 and the associated expectations to 'freeze Europe' in the upcoming winter and then to explore how and why these strategies failed, as most European countries found alternative supplies, while gas prices slowly returned to 2021 levels. Indeed, a class discussion should explicitly address the question of whether Russia's use of the energy weapon can be considered a textbook case of how WI can backfire in the longer-term (see Drezner et al. 2021), given that, by 2024, following the loss of most European markets, Russia's shift toward Eastern customers has been accompanied by a reversal of dependence patterns, particularly reflected in Russia's energy relations with well-diversified China.

On the other hand, the WI concept can be of great pedagogical help to make sense of one of the key elements of Western reactions to Russia's aggression: economic sanctions. Anticipated chokepoint effects of sanctions can be explored at a variety of levels, enabling different groups of students to focus on either 'smart' financial sanctions against Russian oligarchs, export embargoes on high-tech and dual-use goods, or broader sanctions (e.g., oil bans and oil price caps). This can be coupled with the elaboration of the different channels through which these chokepoint effects are meant to reign in Russia's war effort—from the curtailing of the procurement of military equipment to the general weakening of Russia's economy, anticipated to translate into either the exhaustion of Russia's fiscal capacity to fund continued warfare and/or the fueling of domestic discontent in Russian society (see Sonnenfeld et al., 2022).

At the same time, the debate on the limitations of WI strategies allows us to shed systematic light on the controversies around the effectiveness of sanctions in the context of the Russo-Ukrainian war (see Schott, 2023). Here, students can draw on current media reporting to discuss the ways in which Russia has sought to circumvent chokepoint effects, for example, through third-country imports of Western dual-use goods or the partly illicit redirection of oil exports. Broader deterrence effects should also be addressed, as should the question of how sanctions have entailed unintended 'collateral damage' in other parts of the world. Students should be encouraged to assess the question of effectiveness from a comparative perspective, taking into account factors such as target country size and different anticipated time horizons (van Bergejik, 2022). Scenario exercises can be a useful concluding task, allowing students to grapple with the overall question of the impact of Western sanctions on the further trajectory of the Russo-Ukrainian war.

Weaponized interdependence and classroom discussions on international economic order

Beyond allowing to bring in the Russo-Ukrainian war in concrete empirical ways, the WI concept also lends itself well to connecting such insights to broader scholarly and policy debates about the changing nature of the international economic order. In the classroom, this can be explored through a more system-centered and/or through a more actor-centered perspective.

From a systems perspective, one of the most interesting questions to be addressed is whether the Russo-Ukrainian war feeds into a broader transformation that some scholars have conceptualized as the shift from a liberal to a geoeconomic order, whereby core liberal principles like the commitment to global market liberalization and multilateral regulatory frameworks are supplanted by more fragmented economic networks associated with geostrategic spheres of influence ('friendshoring'), accompanied by the decline of international law and institutions such as WTO or IMF (Roberts et al. 2019).

On the one hand, WI strategies can be considered a key indicator of such a shift, and the question of their empirical spread — beyond the Russia-Ukraine conflict itself — can be explored through a range of case studies. On the other hand, students can engage with the broader argument of how fears of anticipated WI strategies fuel fragmentation dynamics; wariness of 'panopticon effects' can be studied through the analysis of communication infrastructures, for example, with regard to satellite technology or submarine cable networks (see Sherman 2021), while fears of chokepoints can be addressed through debates on 'de-risking' in relation to trade and investment flows (see Farrell and Newman 2023). An in-depth case analysis of recent EU-China trade relations can provide particularly compelling material for class discussions. In turn, such discussions can then be related to still more fundamental conceptual and policy questions: Where is the boundary between 'de-risking' and Cold War-style 'de-coupling'? At what point might the securitization of international economic relations, driven by mutual fears of WI, turn into the opposite dynamic that has long underpinned assumptions of liberal interdependence theories, namely that a shift toward the fragmentation of global economic networks might make states less 'invested' in upholding peace and stability?

In a more actor-focused perspective, students can be encouraged to explore the challenges arising from the shift toward a geoeconomic order for liberal democracies. Here, the central question concerns the nature of policy tools to be used—are liberal democracies gradually pursuing WI strategies bound to converge on the 'playing style' (Roberts et al. 2019: 675) of their systemic adversaries, and, if so, what kind of dilemmas does this pose with regard to the possible compromising of liberal principles themselves? Might liberal democracies end up encroaching, both domestically and internationally, on core liberal values and thus inadvertently further imperil the liberal order they purport to defend?

In the context of the Russian invasion, these questions can be addressed in a variety of ways, among which the debate on the freezing and possible seizing of Russian public and private economic assets (see Stephan 2022) provides perhaps the most interesting example. Following the familiarization of students with domestic and international legal frameworks, this theme lends itself well to a formal classroom debate with two groups of students opposing each other, whereby arguments to support asset seizure for Ukrainian reconstruction and broader deterrence can be contrasted with skeptical positions focusing on risks in terms of the compromising of property rights and broader principles of legality and due process, as well as on anticipated negative knock-on effects for international investment confidence. As a concluding follow-up, the analytical potential of the WI concept to outline and illustrate the dilemmas of a geoeconomic order for liberal democracies can be reiterated and linked to analogous dilemmas in other domains, for example, the challenge of how to engage with autocratic disinformation campaigns or the weaponization of irregular migration flows. Teaching IPE in times of war can thus be embedded in a framework that helps to raise awareness of the broader predicament of contemporary liberal societies.

Conclusions

As highlighted at the outset, teaching IPE in the current times of war poses major challenges, and this chapter has only suggested preliminary reflections on some of the ways how this might be done. Whichever way is chosen, broader epistemological and normative difficulties also need to be considered. By way of conclusion, I would like to reflect on two of them: first, the problem that the analysis of the Russo-Ukrainian invasion occurs under conditions of rapid changes on the ground, and second, the unavoidable question of the normative positioning when teaching IPE in times of war.

As much as the overall academic and public engagement with the invasion, IPE-related debates have also been in considerable flux throughout the period since February 2022; this is most easily observed in the controversies around the effectiveness of Western sanctions against Russia, which have oscillated between upbeat assessments in how sanctions will devastate the Russian economy and thus severely constrain the aggressors' warfare capacity (see Sonnenfeld et al. 2022) and extremely pessimistic views of complete failure. For teaching purposes, such oscillations imply the danger of succumbing to analytical insights whose 'half-life' might be very limited. While the contextualization of findings of specific (groups of) authors through a politics of knowledge production approach is always a good tool to 'hedge' such risks, some kind of 'mitigation' attempt will frequently also be warranted, for example, through conscious efforts to highlight different approaches and conclusions.

The normative challenges are no less important. On the one hand, the assumption of a common normative position in terms of the condemnation of Russia's aggression should be made explicit, and the integration of accounts from Ukrainian students about everyday life in war conditions can help to underpin this common 'base.' On the other hand, especially in classrooms that feature a diverse student body originating from countries of the Global

North, Global East, and Global South, views on the causes and consequences of the war, as well as on its importance for global politics, are likely to be different, requiring careful design of classes and teaching material. Concepts with a strong inbuilt normative connotation are better avoided in favor of neutral ones, which, as in the case of WI are suitable for the analysis of the IPE-security nexus regardless of normative views held by different groups of students. At the same time, classroom discussion should also give students occasion to reflect on their own normative views. As outlined above in relation to (neo)liberal and neo-Marxist writing, the explicit engagement with political implications of different intellectual strands of IPE may be conducive to this end. In sum, students should be encouraged to consider a wartime classroom as being inevitably part of a broader politics of knowledge production, yet also to appreciate that this needs to be done in the spirit of academic and political pluralism.

References

Bair, J. et al. (2023), 'RIPE 30th anniversary special feature: looking back and looking forward in IPE', *Review of International Political Economy*, 30 (1): 1-14.

Balaam, D. N. and Dillman, B. (eds., 2019), *Introduction to International Political Economy*, 7th ed., New York: Routledge.

Burawoy, M. (2015), 'Facing an Unequal World', *Current Sociology*, 63 (1): 5-34.

Burlyuk, O. and V. Musliu (eds., 2023), 'The responsibility to remain silent? On the politics of knowledge production, expertise and (self-)reflection in Russia's war against Ukraine', *Journal of International Relations and Development*, 26: 605-18.

Chang, C.C. and A. H. Yang (2020), 'Weaponized Interdependence: China's Economic Statecraft and Social Penetration against Taiwan, *Orbis*, 64 (2): 312-333.

Desai, R. (2013), *Geopolitical Economy: After US hegemony, globalization and empire*, London: Pluto.

Drezner, D.W. et al. (eds., 2021), *The Uses and Abuses of Weaponized Interdependence*, Washington: Brookings Institution Press

Farrell, H. and A. L. Newman (2019), 'Weaponized Interdependence: How Global Economic Networks Shape State Coercion,' *International Security*, 44 (1): 42-79

Farrell, H. and A. L. Newman (2023), 'The New Economic Security State: How De-Risking will remake Geopolitics,' *Foreign Affairs*, 102: 106-17.

Fraser, N. (2014), 'Can Society be Commodities all the way down? Post-Polanyian reflections on capitalist crisis', *Economy and Society*, 43 (4): 541-558.

Gjesvik, L. (2023), 'Private Infrastructure in Weaponized Interdependence,' *Review of International Political Economy*, 30 (2): 722-46.

Godzimirski, J. (ed., 2019), *New Political Economy of Energy in Europe: Power to Project, Power to Adapt*, Cham: Palgrave.

Goldthau, A. and N. Sitter (2015), *A liberal actor in a realist world: The European Union regulatory state and the global political economy of energy*, Oxford: Oxford University Press.

Gowans, S. (2023), 'What's Wrong with the Argument that Russia Isn't Imperialist? A Critique of Desai et al's "The Conflict in Ukraine and Contemporary Imperialism"', in: https://gowans.blog/2023/01/18/whats-wrong-with-the-argument-that-russia-isnt-imperialist-a-critique-of-desai-et-als-the-conflict-in-ukraine-and-contemporary-imperialism/ [accessed on April 26, 2024]

Grigas, A. (2017), *The New Geopolitics of Natural Gas*, Cambridge (Mass.): Harvard University Press

Hall, D. (2022), 'Russias Invasion of Ukraine—a response to David Harvey,' in: https://www.focaalblog.com/2022/02/28/derek-hall-russias-invasion-of-ukraine-a-response-to-david-harvey/ [accessed on April 26, 2024]

Harvey, D. (2005), *The New Imperialism: Clarendon Lectures in Geography and Environmental Studies*, Oxford: Oxford University Press.

Hendl, T. et al. (2023), '(En)Countering epistemic imperialism: A critique of "Westsplaining" and coloniality in dominant debates on Russia's invasion of Ukraine,' *Contemporary Security Policy*, 45 (2): 171-209.

Ikenberry, J. (2018), 'The End of Liberal International Order?', *International Affairs* 94 (1): 7-23.

Mueller, M. (2020), 'In Search of the Global East: thinking between North and South,' *Geopolitics*, 25 (3): 734-55.

Mulder, N. (2022), *The Economic Weapon: The rise of sanctions as a tool of modern war*, New Haven: Yale University Press.

Oatley, T. (eds., 2022), *International Political Economy*, 7th edition, New York: Routledge

Orban, A. (2008), *Power, Energy, and the New Russian Imperialism*, London: Bloomsbury.

Roberts, A. et. al. (2019), 'Toward a Geoeconomic Order in International Trade and Investment', *Journal of International Economic Law*, 22 (4): 655-76.

Rosecrance, R. (1986), *The Rise of the Trading State: Commerce and conquest in the modern world*, London: Basic Books.

Russett, B. (1994), *Grasping the Democratic Peace: Principles for a Post Cold War World*, Princeton: Princeton University Press.

Schott, J. (2023), 'Economic Sanctions against Russia: How Effective, How Durable? *Peterson Institute for International Economics Policy Brief*, 23: 3.

Sherman, J. (2021), *Cyber Defense across the Ocean Floor: The Geopolitics of Submarine Cable Security*, Washington: Atlantic Council.

Siddi, M. (2022), 'EU-Russia energy relations,' in Knodt, M. and M. Kemmerzell (eds.), *Handbook of Energy Governance in Europe*, Cham: Springer, pp. 237-61.

Sonnenfeld, J. et al. (2022), *Business Retreats and Sanctions are Crippling the Russian Economy*, New Haven: Yale School of Management Discussion Paper.

Stephan, P. (2022), 'Seizing Russian Assets,' *Capital Markets Law Journal*, 17 (3): 276-87.

Strange, S. (1994), *States and Markets*, 2nd edition, London: Pinter.

Vakalchuk, R. et. al. (2020), 'Renewable Energy and Geopolitics: A Review', *Renewable and Sustainable Energy Reviews* 122: 1-12.

Van Bergerijk, P. (2022), 'Sanctions against the Russian War on Ukraine: Lessons from History and Current Prospects,' *Journal of World Trade*, 56 (4): 571-86.

Viter, O. et al. (2006), *Ukraine: Post-Revolution Energy Policy and Relations with Russia*, London: GMB Publishing.

From Shock to Adaptation Through National Unity and Action
Third-Year Undergraduate Students of First Eighty Days of Russia's War Against Ukraine

Galyna Solovei

Introduction

The winter semester of the 2021–22 academic year was interrupted in Ukrainian universities by the Russian invasion of Ukraine. At six o'clock in the morning on 24 February 2022, the rector of the Kyiv-Mohyla Academy, Serhiy Kvit, wrote a letter to all faculty, staff, and students of the university informing them that classes were suspended, with a view to allowing them to make decisions directly related to saving their lives and the lives of their families. However, on 9 March, when it became clear that Putin's propaganda slogan about "taking Kyiv in three days" had failed and the attack on the capital had been repelled, online learning resumed at the Kyiv-Mohyla Academy.

One of the courses I teach at the Kyiv-Mohyla Academy in the winter semester is called "Introduction to Peace and Conflict Studies." It provides IR students with the necessary theoretical and methodological framework to analyze the causes, actors, and levels of international violent conflict and outlines the known ways to resolve these conflicts, both diplomatically and through peacekeeping missions, sanctions, and peace enforcement.

Undoubtedly, teaching this course as if the Russian war against Ukraine had never happened and as if neither I nor the 47 students of the course, if not in the bombing zone, had been displaced then inside Ukraine or abroad, would have been a complete abstraction from reality and a sign of my lack of empathy and ability to respond to circumstances. Our lectures and seminars in the academic year of the outbreak of the war, in one way or another, touched upon analyzing the behavior of the aggressor country, non-violent and violent resistance to this aggression in the international arena, the need for military confrontation for self-preservation, and the resilience of Ukrainian society. So, I offered the students an alternative final assignment in the form of an autoethnographic essay about the personal experience of each student facing the war.

In university programs on international security or peace and conflict studies, we focus on actors such as states, international organizations, government and opposition, and organized criminal and terrorist groups. A university professor and their students may often overlook the ordinary person with their experience of living through war. In this study, I build on Christine Silvestre's assertion that understanding the personal experience of war is essential to understanding what war is (Silvestre 2012). I believe that the war can be analyzed not only from the point of view of geopolitics or the struggle for resources but will become more understandable through personal individual stories.

Autoethnography written by students living through the experience of war gives agency to these witnesses of Russian violence, affirming the importance of their testimony and increasing their personal resilience. As Oded Löwenheim puts it, "Autoethnography enables one to acquire an agentive role in the world by highlighting one's uniqueness and voice. It also aims to create mutual empowerment among people, ordinary individuals, by means of identification, connectivity, and empathy" (Löwenheim 2010: 1023). The purpose of this study is to summarize and analyze the personal experiences of Ukrainian students during the first three months of the war. The students described these experiences in their final autoethnographic essays, which became the source of my research data with the students' informed consent. All of the students' essays, written individually, repeated the three themes that

I identified inductively after processing them. These themes became the structural elements of this chapter.

Svetlana Alexievich's book *The Unwomanly Face of War: An Oral History* served as a model for this research. Alexievich writes in the preface that the reality around her was full of stories about the war told by village women, but the entire library was full of books about the heroic deeds of the Soviet army written by men (Alexievich 2017). For years, Alexievich collected Soviet women's testimonies about the Second World War, giving a voice to those who were silenced by the Soviet regime allowing them to heal personal and collective trauma by speaking out. Alexievich had to carefully find each of her interlocutors, build trust between herself and them, and overcome the taboo on the existence and recording of individual stories of the war that differed from the only 'correct' official version approved by the Soviet Communist Party. In the case of the group comprising me as a teacher and the students of my course, we all had more than two years of experience of cooperation and trust between us. The situation in which Russia started the war did not allow any authoritarian force to silence Ukrainian voices or silence any part of society. From 2022 to 2024, hundreds of Western journals in fields ranging from psychology to ecology, law, humanities, and social sciences published special issues of *Ukrainian Voices*, giving Ukrainian scholars and professors a platform to speak out rather than being the object of outside research. With this article, I give a voice to Ukrainian students, as they are an integral part of both Ukrainian society and the teaching and learning process during the war.

While Alexievich's life work overcame the crimes of Soviet authoritarianism by giving a voice to those parts of society whose war stories did not coincide with the official version, Judith Herman, in her book *Trauma and Recovery*, suggests three steps to take to help with traumatic experiences: 1) establish trust and create a safe space; 2) allow the story of the traumatic experience to be told coherently; and 3) restore social ties between group members and the rest of society (Herman 1992). It proved possible to implement this practice through group practical classes for the course "Introduction to Peace and Conflict Studies" in 2021-2022, immediately after the resumption of studies, when students traumatized by the war and scattered around the world easily found "their group" among the fellows and teachers.

In this chapter, I also rely on the work of Israeli researcher Mooli Lahad, who, based on many years of research on war-torn societies, identified the basic adaptation and resilience resources. The BASIC Ph. model, which Lahad developed, is suitable for professor-student interaction during the war. The teacher and students can use the resource sources mentioned by Lahad, such as:

1. B—Belief & values—faith, beliefs, values, philosophy of life.
2. A—Affect—expression of emotions and feelings.
3. S—Socialization—social ties, social support, social belonging, communication.
4. I—Imagination—imagination, dreams, memories, creativity.
5. C—Cognition, thought-mind, cognition, cognitive strategies (Lahad et al. 2012).

Only the last element, Physical, or Ph—as it is called in Lahad's model, could not be used in my course since there was no readily available way for me to actively use the body as a resource for resilience, given that classes were delivered in an online format.

The chapter is structured as follows. First, I present the method used for data collection and analysis. Second, three main themes appearing in most students' essays are introduced, namely: 1) the shock of the outbreak of the war, 2) sensations of unification of the Ukrainian nation, and 3) reactions to family separation. I conclude with recommendations for measures that faculty and students should take to adapt to new circumstances.

The answers to the question "How were you personally affected by the war?" which I and the students, through their essays presented in parts in this study, are aimed at trying to respond to, individualize, and emphasize the personal experience of war. This chapter complements and illustrates the research on the mental health of Ukrainian students conducted using quantitative methods by psychologists (Javanbakht 2022; Kurapov et al. 2022; Osokina et al. 2022; Rogowska and Pavlova 2023). It is worth emphasizing that this study does not aim to analyze the students' mental health from a psychological point of view; rather, it discusses the interaction between a teacher and students who are affected by the war. The ethnographic approach allows us to give students agency in the production of knowledge about the Russian invasion of Ukraine.

Method

Recognizing that my students and I, as a professor, are currently experiencing the traumatic events of the war, that I am a person capable of non-judgmental perception and understanding, and that the students trust me, I encouraged them to structure their traumatic experiences into a coherent story, which in itself brings relief through verbalization. In my opinion, teaching is, to some extent, a participatory research method: we observe the development of our students and correlate our teaching methods depending on their behavior. Participant observation "involves research based on close-up, on-the-ground observation of people and institution in real time and space, in which the investigator embeds herself near (or within) the phenomenon so as to detect how and why agents on the scene act, think and feel the way they do" (Wacquant 2003: 5).

The research was conducted among 47 third-year students of IR at the Kyiv-Mohyla Academy. The students, who come from different parts of Ukraine and were aged 19 or 20, were enrolled in the mandatory course "Introduction to Peace and Conflict Studies" in the 2021–2022 academic year. The main task for the final essay was to produce a free-form description of their personal experience of the first three months of the war. An alternative task was to assess the reaction of Western countries to Russian aggression in Ukraine in the first months of the war. Only seven students from the group decided to complete the alternative task, analyzing the statements and actions of North American and European leaders in January–April 2022. Forty students completed an autoethnographic essay, which demonstrates the students' desire to structure their own experiences and make them "visible" and meaningful to the community.

Nineteen of the 40 students (three males and 16 females) gave written authorization to use parts of their essays for publication under a changed name or their real name without identifying their surnames. The main motivation for students to publish parts of their essays is the desire to ensure that this war is not silenced as it happened with the Holodomor of 1932–33 or with the stories of Soviet women in the World War II of 1939–45. Both orally and in writing, students repeated that they preferred being able to tell and record their own story in their own words to analyzing the official versions of the positions of states or governments that had already been formed or would be formed later as a response to the outcome of the war.

Understanding the entire complex of problems that the students of the Kyiv-Mohyla Academy faced in the first months of the war, I decided to replace the final assignment in the course "Introduction to Peace and Conflict Studies," originally an analytical case study, with an autoethnographic essay, answering the question "How were you personally affected by the war?" Primarily, my task was to point the way to recovery for my students by empowering them to produce a coherent narrative of their own experiences and the shocking events of the war. After analyzing the content of the students' essays, I realized that firsthand testimonies from the participants of the educational process could provide valuable insight for professors and university administrators both in Ukraine and abroad to pay special attention to the challenges that war-affected Ukrainian students may face.

The Shock of the Outbreak of the War

Abraham Maslow, in his theory of human behavior, tried to explain people's motivation to act in one way or another by the hierarchical nature of human needs. According to his theory, only after satisfying the basic needs for food, sleep, shelter, and security can a person be motivated to satisfy higher needs, such as belonging to a community or self-actualization (Maslow 1943). According to this hierarchy, people who suddenly lose the ability to satisfy the basic need for safety and who face physical destruction cannot satisfy any other higher needs until safety is restored.

Loss of security as a result of war can be a traumatic event if it meets three conditions: 1) it is perceived negatively by people; 2) people lose control over the situation; and 3) they were not prepared, and the event occurs suddenly (Carlson & Dalenberg 2000). However, the power of the traumatic effect and the possibility of post-traumatic growth of individuals affected by war or terrorist attacks will not be the same, according to the authors. Five factors that influence people's reaction to trauma are: 1) biological characteristics; 2) developmental level at the time of the trauma; 3) severity of the stressor; 4) social environment; and 5) previous and subsequent life events (Carlson & Dalenberg 2000).

Students describe their reactions to the outbreak of war and the search for satisfaction of the basic need for at least relative security as follows:

> "24th of February, 5 a.m... explosion... I woke up and didn't want to believe what was happening... a few minutes later another loud explosion... I ran to my parents' room... Did it really happen? Is it reality or a dream? This is definitely not a dream...
> In 2 hours, we were already sitting in the car, completely clogged with things, barely fitting, leaving the city. As we drove, we spent every second on the phone, watching the news, and checking every source. We spent 30 hours on the phone, continuing to watch all the news. As soon as we arrived in the Ukrainian Carpathian Mountains, we settled in one room (where the four of us lived for the next few months). For the next few days, we ate almost nothing: we didn't want to. We almost didn't sleep: we didn't want to. We almost didn't get out of bed: we didn't want to. There was complete apathy in every member of the family. But we did not cry. None of us. Why?

We were in a state of shock. We did not fully understand reality. Emotions ceased to exist in us" — Liza.

"At first, you feel like a character in a soap opera and childishly hope that it will be over soon, that someone made a mistake in choosing the show on the streaming service and tomorrow you will be able to return to your 'real' life. It is impossible to believe that it was taken away by abstract people you can't even see. The scenery is filled with a hurriedly turned-on news channel, long car jams outside the window, suitcases packed 'just in case,' and a strange atmosphere of tedious prideful tension in the air. On the same day, rockets began to be fired at my hometown of Kyiv. It was easier to stay within the walls of our dear flat than to go down to the naked basement of a skyscraper building" — Yelisaveta.

"I'm from a small town. All my childhood and youth I wanted to go to the capital and live a better life. But now my soul remains in the half-ruined town that has been under the shots since the beginning of the war. And it is very difficult to realize this. I lived there almost all my life. All victories and troubles are connected with this town" — Olha.

"I remember this feeling of fear and constant anxiety. Sleepless, anxious nights, because every half hour, something explodes so that all the doors, windows, and beds tremble. It was impossible to sleep, so you constantly monitored the news and chatted with friends and relatives. If someone is out of touch for more than an hour, panic begins and you start scrolling through all possible scenarios of what could happen. The worst thing is that it's impossible to stop and distract from what seemed the worst. However, it's only after some time of war that you begin to realize that what you imagined in your head cannot even be compared to the horrible realities of nowadays. The main worries in the beginning were to stock up on food, sit at home with the lights off, and try to figure out how close the explosions were. One day bombs were dropped on my village. Two civilian houses were destroyed, and people were killed and injured. It was scary, but we still didn't know if it would happen again and what should we do. A few days later, I woke up with the news that we were bombed again just as my grandfather went to get groceries. Fortunately, the bomb fell into a ditch and my grandfather was only thrown to one side by a shock wave. He escaped with only a burnt jacket and a minor burn on his hand. But for us, it was the last straw, so we decided to get some things and leave the next day" — Sofia.

"We were there [Irpin] for 10 days. Me, my grandparents, my aunt, uncle, 2 cousins and my cat. The first night was the most stressful. There was an annoying and unstoppable thought in my head that something terrible might happen while we were sleeping. I fall asleep just because I couldn't keep my eyes open anymore. The next few days I was running to the basement every time I heard a bang and I had to take sedatives because after dark I started shaking again and again. Every day we heard explosions and shots. One day we even had to go to the bomb shelter in an old post-Soviet camp. On the last day our friend called and said that a convoy of cars would be going out of Irpin the next day and it was our chance to leave with them. Until the very end, we didn't want to leave. Now, recalling everything, knowing about what happened in Bucha and Irpin afterward, I realize how lucky we were. ...soon after we came [to Warsaw], we found out that my aunt's house (where we were for 10 days in Irpin) was under bomb attack and unfortunately now is almost fully destroyed. My grandparents' house also has some damage but thankfully it's not so serious" — Margaryta.

"My husband is a former military man with experience in participating in the anti-terrorist operation in Donbas. My father came to Kyiv to evacuate us and strangers from my university, who asked for help. I remember that morning minute by minute because it was the day when several russian[1] soldiers entered Kyiv using the stolen Ukrainian tanks. One of them went under our windows. We saw them, people who came to kill us all and bring the 'russian world' to Ukraine. The air raid sirens started. I was scared that my father could have died because of the bombing. On the way out of the city, we were stopped by the Ukrainian military: people with guns and tanks behind. They said that the russian tanks were 10 km from us and we couldn't go this way. We left Kyiv using another road. We relocated to Vinnytsia, my hometown. The next day, we bought some military equipment for my husband, and he went to his parents. He was mobilized and now, he is serving in the Armed Forces of Ukraine" — Maryna.

Two of the key factors of influence are common to the study group, namely, the level of development at the time of the trauma (young people aged 19–20) and the severity of the stressor, which can be considered as serious as possible. Biological characteristics, social environment, and previous and subsequent life events (in addition to studying at the same university) are individual for each student. All the students say that they lived through the beginning of the war with their families; they made the decision to relocate together and experienced the most stressful moments together, which united family members. The unity of the family at the initial stage of the war and the fact that they endured the first attacks together may indicate that the family was the main resource of support and a guarantee of relative security for the individual. Excerpts from the

---

1   Since the beginning of the war, the use of the lower case for "Russia" and "Putin" have become common in the Ukrainian media and academic environment. This phenomenon continues to this day. In Ukrainian, "Russian" would normally be spelt with an initial lower-case "r," but we render it as "russian" here in this translation so as to convey this effect.

autoethnographic essays show that some of the families were ready for relocation, having previously packed their belongings; one of the students' husbands was ready for immediate mobilization to the front. Other students testify to complete surprise and unpreparedness for the outbreak of war, which undoubtedly increases the likelihood of more serious trauma. All the students, even those who survived the occupation in Irpin, say that they cannot complain because they are much more fortunate than others. Having relocated, students begin to feel relatively safe. After a few months of war, the understanding of a critical level of danger in which one cannot live anymore is transferred exclusively to the front line and the occupied territories. The rest of Ukraine is perceived as conditionally safe, even under the constant shelling.

Unity of Ukrainians. Volunteering. Working for Ukrainian Victory

Resilience is generally defined as the ability of an individual to "bounce back" after experiencing stress (Wald et al. 2006). People can thrive while their known world crumbles around them (*Resilience and Trauma – The BASIC Ph Model – Brighton Therapy Partnership*). After the shock reaction, various strategies of adaptation to the changed living conditions come into play. People with higher adaptability, which is an innate quality (biological factor) or a consciously developed skill, can find resources and move on to the post-traumatic growth phase. The most famous phrase attributed to Charles Darwin, but which he did not record in his books, proclaims that "It is not the strongest of the species that survive, nor the most intelligent, but the one most responsive to change" (Darwin Correspondence Project n/d). This statement reflects the importance of adaptability in the face of evolutionary challenges. For Ukrainian society, the Russian invasion was just such a challenge, and to survive, Ukrainians demonstrated an unprecedented level of cohesion, unity, and desire to fight the enemy. After three months of war, students described their experiences as follows:

"You wake up with only one thing in mind — to be valuable to your nation. You crowd-fund for the cars that will soon be destroyed in combat on the frontline, order tourniquets to save the lives of your soldiers; you help people relocate as they are fleeing from the genocide, and you bury yourself in work so as not to feel like a liability" — Tetyana.

"Of course, we have all come to terms with the war and we do everything to accelerate the onset of our victory. All those who are in safety should help our army, the soldiers who are protecting us every day. My dad and I organized some deliveries of humanitarian aid from Poland. We have a truck, and my father agreed to load the humanitarian aid in Poland that we brought here and handed over to volunteers" — Illya.

"My family was in Ukraine for the first 10 days of the war. We spent most of those days in the bomb shelter. Despite the danger, these were the most impressive days of my life. I have never seen such cohesion. We helped each other, we tried to make life easier for everyone. The whole yard, all my neighbors in the morning and afternoon were preparing food for our volunteers and the army in a restaurant nearby. Before the war, I had never communicated with my neighbors so sincerely and openly. I had no idea how wonderful my neighbors were. I think the war has shown how much people, in particular the Ukrainian people, united by one problem, can create such great things and create such synergies" — Kateryna.

"Being a teacher for adults was not easy before the war. Being a teacher for adults while there is war in your country was unbearable. What can we discuss? What can I ask? What if someone has lost something valuable? What if they start crying? What if I say something wrong? And the neverending list of 'what ifs' that didn't let you be the same person you were before. It felt like I had lost the ability to communicate with people. The boundaries between what's right and what's wrong got blurred and you question every word you say and every move you make. Asking quite a regular 'before' question like 'What's your favorite place to eat out?' made one of my students from Kharkiv burst into tears 'after'... their favorite place was burnt down to ashes. Nevertheless, I realized that I was doing something right. A lot of my students used our lessons to prepare for the interviews for foreign media to spread awareness about what's truly happening in Ukraine. Others asked me to help translate articles and videos to let the world know about our courage. I might not be able to fight holding a gun, but I help Ukrainians to raise their voices and make the whole world hear and understand us" — Olha.

"When the war broke out again, I wanted to be as useful to Ukraine as possible. I was not in shape to be a soldier, I never had substantial experience with volunteering in person, and I could not go abroad to buy thermal imagers and bulletproof vests because I did not even have a driving license. The only thing I knew I could for sure do was writing — and that is how the idea of 'Mediaoffensive' project came to my mind. I gathered a group of 36 students of international relations and political science, and we started contacting media outlets and newspapers abroad, offering them our help in covering the war in Ukraine. Our goal was simple. We wanted to ensure that foreign readers would get objective, comprehensive, and timely reporting about what was happening in our country. We wrote analytical articles, recorded interviews, told personal stories, contacted experts for exclusive commentary, and more. As of now, we have eleven partners from seven countries in Europe and Northern America. We work with them regularly and on a volunteer basis, and we hope that our contributions raise awareness about the Russian war in Ukraine among foreigners" — Anhelina.

"While coping with aggressive sentiments towards people justifying war crimes and the brutal invasion of my Homeland, I started participating in protests and campaigns concerning awareness-raising in cooperation with the Ukrainian diaspora in Scotland which appeared to be the most natural move since I became a relocated Ukrainian in my 20s. Just as it is always described in modern psychological research, a common goal, and a common enemy bind people together and ease the consequences of the collective trauma respectively. We managed to implement a multi-stage action plan in order to keep reminding local people and media as well that civilians and young children in Ukraine are suffering from an improbable outbreak of violence that should be broadcast everywhere to show some real evidence to those brainwashed. To be honest, it was never an easy goal to reach however we experienced an advantage as representatives of the University community therefore people around us were in favor of receiving our viewpoint. We were protesting in other Scottish towns occasionally and I then accidentally became a coordinator of a Ukrainian society at the University of Glasgow which was established sometime before and regained its potential in 2022 when it was needed at most. In cooperation with the 'Mediaoffensive' initiative that provided us with the required materials for publishing and engaging people to join our efforts, we launched a fundraising campaign for displaced families within Ukraine to support them with necessary supplies and a safe place to stay" — Nivena.

"As soon as I arrived in Germany, I threw myself into volunteering at the main railway station. In the smallest amount of time, with the chaos engulfed because of the nonexistent coordinated and prepared help for Ukrainians, as mostly everything had been run by the small local volunteer groups and consolers. With my knowledge of Ukrainian, Russian, and English with a little German that I had scratched from the lessons back in my school days, I have found myself useful. There were so many people with lost relatives, so many heartbroken women with children rushing to any available volunteer for help, so many cries of old people who don't have anything left after their long and fruitful life except two bags of clothes and one file with documents. And so many young girls and underage boys without parents, came here because their parents were worried sick if they hadn't fled the country. The first few weeks were the worst ones" — Nguen.

Regarding the involvement of students of this course in volunteer activities and the quality of their studies, it is worth noting three main points. A small number of students found much more meaning in volunteer activities and struggle, which completely diverted their attention and efforts from the educational process. The quality of their academic performance deteriorated, but their mental health was good. A greater share of students managed to combine volunteering, especially at foreign universities, with high academic performance. Here, it is worth noting the highly positive impact of the openness of partner universities of the Kyiv-Mohyla Academy, which accepted Ukrainian students for semester and year studies after the beginning of the invasion and strongly supported student initiatives. A large proportion of students began to experience problems with mental health and decreased motivation to study, unable to cope with stress on their own. Undoubtedly, factors that cannot be revealed through autoethnographic essays, such as biological characteristics or preceding events in each student's life before the Russian invasion, contributed to this. However, the student essays do reveal one powerful factor, namely, family separation, which appears to be crucial to the deterioration of resilience and adaptability to the constant stress of war.

Student Desperation over Family Separation

Israeli professor Mooli Lahad, whose goal was to develop methods to increase the resilience of people living in conflict zones, developed a model of coping with stress based on thousands of cases, which he called the Basic Ph Model. Below, I will describe how I adapted Lahad's model for teaching during the war, without including the Ph, which is the use of bodily resources to cope with the stress of war and which I felt was impossible to apply in the case of an online course.

B — belief

The belief, in this case, is not only faith in God but also unquestioning confidence in the 'power' of the students' parents and extended family, who constantly cared for and protected them. Another shared belief of Ukrainian students before the Russian invasion was the belief in the power of international organizations and the belief in the rule of law, and the ability of the international community to stop Russian aggression. Even in the third month of the war, student essays demonstrate the value of unity among Ukrainians and the belief in Ukraine's victory with the help of international partners.

A — affect

Emotions, such as fear, anger, disgust, and confusion, which an individual can express and find legitimization for in society, facilitate the perception of traumatic experience, do not 'drive' it into the trauma of the generation, and make it "felt," "expressed," and "experienced together." Having empathetic people around the students who allowed them to experience emotions and respond to these emotions correctly, without trying to "force happiness," allowed students to increase their resilience.

S — social

This strategy builds on the previous one by emphasizing the strengthening of social ties, such as friendships, hobby clubs, informal connections within the student body, and communication with teachers. An individual's isolation during the stress of war almost negates their resilience. In terms of this strategy, the resumption of studies at the Kyiv-Mohyla Academy just two weeks after the start of the invasion played an important positive role in restoring a sense of belonging to the students and faculty.

I — imagination

Creativity and imagination help individuals experiencing constant stress to find strength and express emotions through art, writing, drama, dance, and song. The students' readiness and willingness to write an autoethnographic essay in a free creative style instead of analytical research amid war and the free and supportive way of discussing traumatic experiences in the classroom are very positive experiences in my teaching.

C — cognitive

A cognitive strategy for overcoming traumatic experiences involves discussing in a group and thinking about solutions to the problem the individual is struggling with in several ways. Without a doubt, the high individual cognitive qualities of students, professors, mentors, and teachers working with students from the conflict zone should use more group assignments, where the wisdom of the group and the joint search for the best way to solve a problem increases the resilience of each group member.

Most of Lahad's resilience-building strategies emphasize finding support in the group's shared values, empathy for emotions, and joint development of problem-solving strategies. The isolation of an individual, exclusion from the group, and loneliness in the face of the horrors of war make them particularly vulnerable to trauma. The main social groups for students are their family, friends, and university communities.

Three types of family separation are highlighted in the student essays: 1) The student goes abroad, and the family remains in Ukraine in "relative safety," which, as noted above, means being at risk of Russian bombing, albeit not on the occupied territory and not on the frontline; 2) Separation of the family in Ukraine, when a student goes to its safest western part, leaving parents in the central, eastern, northern or southern part of Ukraine; 3) Separation from extended multinational family, when Russian relatives are no longer the usual support for students, but become enemies.

Students who, thanks to the support of the Kyiv-Mohyla Academy, their own or their parents' efforts, had the opportunity to leave Ukraine to study abroad during the first days of the war felt much worse than if they had gone to such study as planned. Miriam George distinguishes between anticipatory and acute refugees, noting that acute refugees suffer much more than those migrants who planned their journey (George 2009). Even the previously planned mobility to Germany, which guaranteed the student a safe stay, was perceived by her as very stressful under the conditions of the war because it involved the separation of the family, during which the parents would have to remain in the attacked territory. Similarly, moving to a safer place inside Ukraine, with the condition that their parents would be in danger, caused much stress for the students.

> "The decision to relocate was not an easy one to make, but practically it was much easier for me to embody it than for many other people who had nowhere to go. A few months before the invasion I was accepted for international mobility to the university in Germany. By the end of February, I had a visa, health insurance, and a place to stay, as well as tickets for the flight on the 1st of April. My parents were glad that my residency was figured out, however, I was thinking a lot about whether I should leave or not. I have been waiting for a chance to experience studying and living abroad for a long time, but the ambiguity of circumstances spoke for itself. The 'survivor's guilt' followed me for a long time as I was weighing up rational and irrational reasons to stay or to leave. After all, I agreed with my parents on the reasonability of going rather than staying" — Yuliya.

> "Right now, I'm 2000 kilometers away from my family. They're in Kyiv, I'm in France. When I was saying goodbye to them, a big part of me stayed there. I clenched my fists and gritted my teeth just not to cry in front of them. The moment I left I couldn't stop the tears. My only wish is to see them again, healthy and happy" — Anna.

> "When on the morning of the seventh day of the war we were preparing to say our goodbyes, my father went to another room and there he had a panic attack. My mother was reassuring him saying that it was nice that I was leaving because I would be safe. When he came out, for the first time in my life I saw my father crying. I sat on the couch and finished my breakfast. Mom came over. I joked about something. She looked at me and said that I should not hide my feelings. I said nothing. Going out into the street to go to the car, I looked at our farm. The pain was sharp. I felt like thousands of eyes were looking at me waiting for me to cry. I wanted to cry so badly that

in order not to do this I had to strain every cell of my body. I hugged my parents. They were crying. I was not. A family friend and I sat in the car. I smiled at my parents through the window. We passed through the gate, drove out into the street, and headed towards the exit from the village. I thought that now I would finally cry when my parents could not see me, but I did not. Something seemed to break in me, and this breakdown allowed me to feel a saving numbness. What worried me least of all at that moment was my own future fate" — Kateryna.

"My parents called a family council and told me and my boyfriend looking straight into the pupils of our eyes that we should save ourselves and leave alone without them. At first, I didn't believe what they said and denied it. But then my parents convinced us, and we left for Vasylkiv to stay with my boyfriend's dad, to spend the night there and go to western Ukraine the next day. This happened on March 8. While we were driving to Vasylkiv, we were stopped at a military post and the guys from the territorial defense gave me the most beautiful tulip I had ever seen and asked my boyfriend, smiling: 'Are you taking all the pretty girls out of Kyiv?' This way they congratulated me on International Women's Day. As soon as we left the military post, tears streamed down my cheeks, and I couldn't hold back my sobs. Because I was very touched that our defenders, despite the darkness around them, remembered an echo of peaceful life, a holiday I was sure everyone had forgotten about" — Maria. "Our relatives who have lived in Russia for several decades stopped being our family. We never thought that adults, who we thought were intelligent people, turned out to be zombies without any logical sense. Again 'why?' Maybe because it's easier to be stupid or it's the destiny of Russian civilians, to let someone control their minds and lives" — Anna.

"Once I saw a familiar Russian phone number on the screen, I immediately thought of the aim of the phone call—I expected an offer of help, apologies or mere sympathy. My expectations broke into pieces the exact moment I picked up the phone and heard the question 'How are you doing, khokhols?' [khohols—a derogatory term used by Russians towards Ukrainians to highlight the inferiority of the Ukrainian nation in comparison with the Russian one—GS] in a highly ironic tone. As it turned out, the purpose of the call was mocking the situation my family had got into, blaming Ukrainians for the beginning of the 'military operation' and threatening us with a Russian superior army. While being shocked and extremely emotional, I was not able to control myself under the given circumstances and, obviously, could not tolerate such statements. Quite predictably, our fight further escalated into a scandal—and I decided to never talk to my relatives again. Having heard how disrespectful and ignorant they were towards their own relatives and how desperately they tried to justify Russia's actions, I caught myself thinking that I am unlikely to forgive them" — Valeria.

"Like many other Ukrainians, I had (not sure I can say "have" anymore) many close family members in Russia, unfortunately for us all in Moscow. I spent the first three weeks waiting for a text from them—my little cousin couldn't forget about me, could she? We spent so many years together, kids with only a two-year difference, being proud of how we could understand each other when no one else could. But the day came when this understanding irreversibly cracked—the day when I saw a picture of her smiling at the concert commemorating the anniversary of Crimea's annexation. Covered all in Russian flags, with the letter 'Z' on her chest. This is how I broke all of my connections with anything Russian apart from the language. I am Ukrainian, but I still speak Russian in my family" —Natalia.

Students whose families did not split, either by going abroad together or staying together in a "relatively safe place" in Ukraine, and those students who had separated from the Russian part of their extended family before the full-scale invasion, showed significantly more resilience in their autoethnographic essays.

Conclusion

The resumption of studies at the Kyiv-Mohyla Academy on 9 March 2022, just two weeks after the start of the Russian invasion of Ukraine, has preserved the students' and faculty's sense of belonging to the university community, which has greatly increased our resilience and ability to withstand the stress of war. The nature of this war, namely its recognition by both Ukrainian and international society as an unprovoked, illegitimate invasion and not a "special military operation to Ukraine," as Russian propaganda insists, makes it possible not to silence the daily experience of war of Ukrainians, as it was in the Soviet Union, but to speak about it, meeting with understanding among the international community. This speaking out and the understanding of the world community in response removes the stigma of guilt and shame from the victim of aggression for being attacked.

The analysis of autoethnographic essays by third-year students in the IR program at the Kyiv Mohyla Academy, in which they described their experiences of the first three months of the war, revealed that all students, without exception, experienced the shock of the overwhelming violence at the start of the war. The main factors of this experience, felt by the students as traumatic, were the suddenness of the attack, the inability to control the situation, and the huge scale of violence and destruction. Despite the harshness of the situation, family ties, the unity of the Ukrainian people in resisting the aggressor, involvement in volunteer activities, and a sense of belonging to the university community acted as pillars that allowed students to increase resilience in critical situations. Meanwhile, separation from their families and alienation from Russian relatives who fully supported Russia's "special military operation" against Ukraine, therefore, against their own blood relatives, feature as the factors that bring the most suffering to students.

It is worth realizing that factors that affect resilience, such as biological features, events preceding or following the stress in the life of each student, and the severity of losses of each of them, are beyond the control of professors and the university administration. At the same time, professors should be aware that a cohort of students who already have built trust among themselves and with the professor is one of the most important groups from which students can draw resources for resilience. Adapting the resource-oriented model of Mooli Lahad to the university environment, professors can use the following tools: 1) emphasizing shared beliefs and common values; 2) providing opportunities to share negative emotions and being able to respond to them empathetically; 3) ensuring that none of the students remains isolated, to promote the creation and maintenance of social connections among students; 4) using imagination and creativity in individual assignments, and 5) using problem-solving teamwork.

References

Alexievich, S. (2017) *The Unwomanly Face of War: An Oral History of Women in World War II*, trans. Richard Pevear and Larissa Volokhonsky. Penguin Books.

Darwin Correspondence Project. (n/d) *Six Things Darwin Never Said — And One He Did. Darwin Correspondence Project.* https://www.darwinproject.ac.uk/people/about-darwin/six-things-darwin-never-said.

George, M. (2009) A Theoretical Understanding of Refugee Trauma, *Clinical Social Work Journal* 38(4) (December): 379-87.

Herman, J. (1992) *Trauma and Recovery*. New York: Basic Books.

Javanbakht, A. (2022) "Addressing War Trauma in Ukrainian Refugees Before it is Too Late," *European Journal of Psychotraumatology* 13(2) (5 August).

Kurapov, A., Pavlenko, V., Drozdov, A., Bezliudna, V., Reznik, A., and Isralowitz, R. (2022) "Toward an Understanding of the Russian-Ukrainian War Impact on University Students and Personnel," *Journal of Loss and Trauma* (13 June): 1–8.

Lahad, M., Leykin, D., Krkeljic, L., Rogel, R., & Lev, Y. (2012) *BASIC Ph Model of Coping and Resiliency: Theory, Research, and Cross-Cultural Application*. Kingsley Publishers.

Löwenheim, O. (2010) "The 'I' in IR: An Autoethnographic Account," *Review of International Studies* 36(4) (13 July): 1023–45.

Meadows, S., Miller, L., and Robson, S. (2015) "Understanding Resilience," in *Airman and Family Resilience: Lessons from the Scientific Literature*. RAND Corporation, 9–22.

Osokina, O., Silwal, S., Bohdanova, T., Hodes, M., Sourander, A., and Skokauskas, N. (2022) "Impact of the Russian Invasion on Mental Health of Adolescents in Ukraine," *Journal of the American Academy of Child & Adolescent Psychiatry* (October)

Rogowska, A. M., and Pavlova, I. (2023) "A Path Model of Associations between War-related Exposure to Trauma, Nightmares, Fear, Insomnia, and Posttraumatic Stress among Ukrainian Students during the Russian Invasion," *Psychiatry Research* 328 (October): 115431.

Semerikov, S., Vakaliuk, T., Mintii, I. and Didkivska, S. (2023) "Challenges facing Distance Learning during Martial Law: Results of a Survey of Ukrainian Students," *Educational Technology Quarterly* (7 October).

Sylvester, C. (2013) *War As Experience: Contributions from International Relations and Feminist Analysis*. Taylor & Francis Group.

Wacquant, L. (2003) "Ethnografeast: A Progress Report on the Practice and Promise of Ethnography." *Ethnography* 4, № 1: 5–14. https://doi.org/10.1177/1466138103004001001.

Wald, J., Taylor, S., Asmundson, G. J., Jang, K. L., & Stapleton, J. (2006). *Literature Review of Concepts: Psychological Resiliency* (No. DRDCCR-2006-073). British Columbia University Vancouver.

An Essay from a Rector
The Challenges and Rewards of Teaching During Wartime

Tymofii Brik

War is an unparalleled tragedy and hardship that anyone can experience. Despite its profound challenges, this invasion also presents new opportunities for educators. As a researcher, educator, and citizen who has lived through the Russian invasion while remaining in Kyiv, I have witnessed first-hand the critical role of education in shaping a nation's resilience.

This war targeted Ukrainian identity and culture, as well as educational institutions—schools, museums, theaters, and universities. According to estimates by the KSE Institute, as of January 2024, the infrastructure of education has suffered damage amounting to $6.8 billion (KSE Institute, 2024). This includes hundreds of schools and kindergartens, as well as university labs and facilities, which were shelled. Many scholars and students were displaced, both internally and abroad. Some surveys suggest that around 18.5% of Ukrainian scientists had left by the autumn of 2022, with many of these emigrant scientists being among the most productive researchers in Ukraine (De Rassenfosse 2023). However, many of these migrant scientists are employed by their host universities on insecure contracts. About 15% of the scientists who remained in Ukraine have stopped conducting research, and the remaining scientists have seen their research time significantly reduced. Many of those who stayed were not able to physically reach their institutions or have lost access to crucial data for their studies (Rassenfosse 2023). More recent data suggest that a total of 12% of Ukrainian researchers working in the public sector have been forced to relocate (6.3% have emigrated, and 5.5% have been internally displaced), while 30% of researchers have been forced to work remotely

(UNESCO 2024). In terms of output, research papers produced by Ukrainian scientists declined by about 10% (Ganguli and Waldinger 2024).

While the above estimates and data illustrate the tangible damages of war, one must also bear in mind the intangible and human aspects of this tragedy. Many of us lost friends, loved ones, colleagues, and students. Many faculty members and students volunteered to serve as medics or soldiers, became volunteers, or were mobilized by the state. In her last email, one of my students, Iryna Tsybukh, who volunteered as a medic, expressed her hope to finish her MA thesis, which focused on the politics of national memory in Ukraine, once the victory was won. Tragically, she lost her life while evacuating casualties from the frontline in 2024. My co-author, Oleksiy Shestakovsky, perhaps the only sociologist in Ukraine who truly understands the intricacies of structural equation models, is bravely defending us on the front lines. Instead of publishing his papers in top journals, he is fulfilling his duty to protect Ukraine and other democracies.

This personal experience resonates with national sociological surveys. Some early longitudinal polls revealed that the total number of people affected by the war in any way grew from 20% to 80%, while 84% said they knew someone at the front (Alekseev and Dembitskyi 2024a, 2024b). Despite these horrors, most Ukrainians have shown significant resilience. The number of people who identify as Ukrainian has risen from about 60% to 80%, and trust in the president and government has increased significantly, alongside trust in the military and volunteers[1]. Most notably, local communities and governance have demonstrated remarkable resistance and adaptability in the face of war (Rabinovych et al. 2023). However, such resilience cannot be sustained indefinitely. Sociologists have ob-

---

1 Kyiv International Institute of Sociology. Report about the public opinion after 10 months of the invasion. https://kiis.com.ua/?lang=ukr&cat=reports&id=1175&page=1

served a decline in trust in formal institutions after two years of invasion. Nevertheless, trust in the military and a certain degree of optimism persist.

Nevertheless, the war is also a unique time for social and personal mobilization, for unity and compassion, and even for growth. Many institutions in Ukraine, which were previously perceived as failing, have shown their best during the most challenging times. One example is the national railway. Once heavily criticized by citizens for poor service and an outdated spirit, the railways became national heroes, moving and evacuating displaced populations, facilitating logistics during the war, delivering humanitarian aid, and even bringing top international diplomats to Kyiv. The same can be said about national procurement, the National Bank, seaports that manage export operations, and many other institutions (for more discussion on the state of institutions in Ukraine, see Brik et al. 2024).

One of the most crucial institutions that sustained itself during the attack on Ukrainian culture and identity is the university. Universities became centers of community during the attacks, served as diplomatic hubs to support international ties and assist migrants, and became centers for research and defense innovations. They have also remained vital in sustaining human capital[2].

Reflecting on my personal experiences, the KSE (where I served as a researcher, wartime VP for international affairs, and later as rector) has truly embraced the power of a university to instill hope and provide a future for the country through defense, education, and rebuilding efforts. In the first months of the invasion, we remained in Kyiv, investing in building shelters, purchasing generators and Starlinks, as well as other necessary equipment. Our

---

2   See more in the work of Nathan Greenfield, who reported on this matter extensively: "War has not dampened Ukrainian scholars' courage to think" (University World News, 18 July 2024). "Universities join forces to help save body, mind and spirit" (University World News, 20 February 2024). "A year of war: Counting the psychosocial cost for students" (University World News, 29 March 2023).

admission numbers remained relatively stable, with only a 10% decrease compared to the previous year. This is in stark contrast to other Ukrainian universities, which saw drops of up to 50% in admissions. Back then, our KSE Foundation was recognized as one of the top 50 charitable organizations in Ukraine, receiving the prestigious Golden Heart award from the president of Ukraine. By 2024, KSE University witnessed a remarkable 3.5-fold increase in enrollment, growing to 750 students, alongside the launch of eight innovative programs. Our students raised over $2 million for medical evacuation helicopters, delivering two so far, with three more on the way. The KSE Foundation gathered nearly $120 million for humanitarian support in Ukraine, while our research unit, the KSE Institute, undertook significant government projects supporting the economy, securing international funding, and advancing Ukraine's preparation for EU integration. Based on this experience, I feel confident in my position to comment on university management during the war. Perhaps this chapter can offer some valuable reflections on Ukraine's experience and provide insights for those in academia.

More specifically, I would like to stress the growing role of IR for the Ukrainian nation as well as for our university. IR, a crucial discipline for studying the dynamics of power and diplomacy, has long been neglected in Ukraine. However, with the onset of the Russian invasion, the government, NGOs, and activists have clearly realized how important international diplomacy is for building trust, generating support, and presenting Ukrainian narratives about the war.

Moreover, many intellectuals have argued that Ukraine's absence from the international global agenda (including academia) and its peripheral role in diplomacy had a profoundly negative impact on Ukraine's position vis-à-vis Russia in the first place. Furthermore, Ukraine did not have sufficient institutional support to advocate for its narratives and needs. Arguments were often not based on rigorous research, and the framing of these arguments failed to align with globally accepted standards.

Thus, IR is essential in its practical and performative roles. Practically, Ukraine lacked the "practice of IR," meaning active participation in state-of-the-art diplomacy and academic exchange. Performatively, Ukrainian representatives lacked the concepts, models, and language to communicate effectively. This gap led to critical mistakes in relations with the Global South, as well as inefficiencies in securing support from the West. As an example, on a local level, few scholars or public intellectuals were able to effectively engage with figures like John Mearsheimer in debates to advocate for the Ukrainian point of view. Which inevitably weakened Ukrainian's position in the global dialogue.

Given all this, our university needed to invest in IR in its various forms — from teaching selected courses in IR, European integration, global democracy, and authoritarian regimes to building new ties with diplomats and embassies. These varied actions were essential to embedding IR as a core part of the university's intellectual framework.

In what follows, I will focus on our general approaches, which can be applied to IR or any other discipline.

Incubating Talent

One of the key lessons I learned is that human capital truly matters — a seemingly trivial observation but one that is crucial during war. Talented and motivated individuals will find ways to support themselves and their communities. The role of a university is to support these individuals by providing safety, psychological support, and opportunities to excel in what they do best. We organized the "Ukrainian Global University" to incubate talent — not just to offer temporary shelter but to provide full degrees, enabling these individuals to return and contribute to rebuilding Ukraine through work in government or business. In 2022, we received almost 1000 applications and selected 200 participants from the UGU. Only 56 of them were placed in international universities (NYU Prague,

Paris School of Economics, Paris-1, IE Madrid, City University London, UMASS Amherst, University of Toronto). Some of these students have already returned, like Victoriia Severym, who works in the field of public policy after receiving her MA in Mank School, Toronto. This example is especially relevant for the current chapter since Mank School has accepted a few of our students to their MA program, Global Affairs (MGA), which aims to improve Ukraine's capacity in IR.

We also immediately launched online classes for our students — our experience with COVID-19 allowed us the flexibility to adapt quickly. Three months later, we resumed in-person education on our campus in Kyiv after constructing reliable bomb shelters with underground classrooms. This was important because students were seeking a sense of fundamental fulfillment. They wanted to study, to be close to each other, and to prove to themselves and others that they were resilient. From 2022 to 2025, the total number of students at KSE increased from about 250 to 1100. This increase happened due to our commitment to safety (studies continued with no interruptions in shelters), the launch of new programs (some of them had a new focus on security, global order, European integration and other similar topics crucial for IR), and also donations. The foundation became one of the top five in Ukraine, according to *Forbes* magazine in 2024. Despite its focus on humanitarian aid, the KSE Foundation also supported talented students with tuition fees and accommodation, which helped us to increase enrollment.

The same can be said about our scholars. Many of our faculty members became volunteers, but they never stopped being scholars. They wanted to continue thinking and writing papers as a way to sustain their integrity and humanity while also contributing to applied sciences. Although many international partners offered programs like "Scholars at Risk," encouraging our faculty to move to safer places, most of our faculty chose to remain in Ukraine, close to their families and communities, while continuing their scientific work. This sentiment aligned with earlier surveys among displaced

Ukrainians, who expressed a strong willingness to return home when the opportunity arises[3].

We also partnered with UMass and George Washington University to offer non-residential fellowships. Our networks and early surveys among scholars indicated that many Ukrainians chose to remain in Ukraine and needed support. The non-resident scholarships proved to be highly effective. While organizing these fellowships logistically and legally was challenging, we leveraged our infrastructure—we have a foundation registered in Washington, D.C., dual degree programs with the University of Houston, and an international academic board to ensure credibility, financial accountability, and the capacity to absorb and redistribute support.

Capacity Matters

This point leads to another important observation: organizational structure and capacity matter. Many international agencies and donors perceived the situation of education and science in Ukraine through the common ideological and bureaucratic lens of public institutions versus private institutions. Many agencies refused to help KSE because we were perceived as a private university, based on the assumption that public universities need support while private ones can find their own resources in the market. This lens proved inaccurate. In fact, private universities like KSE and Ukrainian Catholic University managed to offer more public goods. Given our international structure, experience, and capacity, we were able to absorb aid and distribute it effectively. Public universities, on the other hand, were often constrained by government bureaucracy and lacked the experience and skills (sometimes even English proficiency) needed to navigate this environment.

To expand our support to include public universities, KSE and UCU created the "Alliance of Universities," which now includes two private universities, four public universities, and two public

---

[3] Regular surveys of migrants were executed by Gradus (https://gradus.app/en/open-reports/future-ukraine-gradus-research-ukr/)

"associate members." This alliance ensures that we can support both public and private institutions. The lesson here is that Ukraine, like many other countries, has its unique context, and in times of war, the most reliable way to provide help is to identify capable and credible local partners with knowledge of the local context and experience in deploying projects. Such institutions, regardless of whether they are public or private, will be able to facilitate and expand support to others.

Relevance Is the Key

Another important point is that specialization and institutional foundations are less relevant during wartime compared to the importance of relevance. The KSE was initially perceived as a small private university focused solely on economics. However, during the war, we launched innovative programs in psychology, law, urban science, and cybersecurity. We also established a new School of Engineering with two experimental MA programs in drone building and microelectronics, as well as new departments in mathematics and theoretical physics. How did an 'economics' university evolve into one offering programs in psychology and microelectronics? Initially, most donors and partners were skeptical. They recognized that fundamental science is important, but they misallocated funds to traditional universities that ultimately failed to deliver.

Our main strategy and motivation were to move beyond our own limitations and expand into areas that were relevant to the country's needs. How did we determine what was relevant? First, our own KSE Institute researched war damage and identified that housing infrastructure was the most severely impacted. This implied that someone would need to rebuild the cities once the war ended. Surveys showed that many Ukrainians were experiencing stress and anxiety, including war-related nightmares. As a result, we needed to launch programs in psychology to address trauma. Ukrainian and international politicians quickly began discussing

European integration, which created a demand for lawyers to train the next generation of negotiators and European integration experts. Additionally, we needed lawyers to address Russia's war crimes in international courts.

Additionally, we focused on what everyone else needed. Alignment with broader societal needs is the best way to navigate the unpredictability and fog of war. International donors, missions, and politicians, along with local businesses and citizens, all expressed interest in security, logistics, agriculture, and innovation. Therefore, we had no choice but to move in these directions by launching new programs and hiring new faculty. We managed to attract talented students. In 2024, the highest standardized test scores were among UCU, KSE, and Kyiv Mohyla Academy. We managed to grow without sacrificing quality, and the key was identifying and offering relevant programs.

In terms of serving our mission for "IR in practice," our team has consistently generated reports that were put into practice by international governments and non-government actors. For instance, the KSE Institute has produced various reports and analytics on sanctions toward Russia, including reports on the shadow fleet. Most recently, the KSE Institute published a groundbreaking report uncovering significant ties between the Russian Psychological Society (RPS) and the Kremlin (KSE Institute 2025). It highlights how the RPS promotes state narratives, militarizes society, and influences international psychological associations and networks[4]. This is an example of the "IR in practice," which defends the position of Ukraine in the international arena and shows how Russian military, political, and scientific institutions are interconnected in pushing war propaganda and false narratives about politics and culture.

---

4   https://sanctions.kse.ua/wp-content/uploads/2025/01/The-Russian-Psychological-Society-After-2022_-Serving-the-State-Shaping-Ideology-Weaponizing-Science.pdf

A New University

Finally, a university is not just a harbor where talents can be saved and incubated; it is also an agent of change with agency and political power. In times of war, society entertains different, if not dangerous, ideas and ideologies. Government and society became more centralized and mobilized around the ideas of security and nationalism. This raises many questions: What is the best policy for local governance—centralization or decentralization? How do we balance economic needs with military recruitment? What is the role of freedom of speech in an environment filled with disinformation and propaganda? All these questions have significant moral dilemmas and consequences. However, the only place to truly debate them is within a university, which can offer methodology and neutrality to minimize conflicts and polarization while ensuring that discussions are grounded in data and arguments.

While regional universities suffer under authoritarian regimes (Russian top universities have become sterile, and Viktor Orbán harassed the Central European University), we aim to build the future of Ukraine by creating a truly global university in the region that will uphold democratic values and foster growth for the next generation. It is a romanticized idea, but it keeps us motivated during the darkest times.

In conclusion, the invasion has tested us in unimaginable ways, yet it has also revealed the profound resilience and adaptability of our institutions and people. The KSE, once a specialized institution, has evolved to meet the pressing needs of a nation under siege, demonstrating that relevance and responsiveness are key in times of crisis. Our experience underscores that universities are not just centers of learning; they are vital agents of change, capable of leading society through its most challenging moments. As we continue to navigate the uncertainties of war, we remain committed to our mission—nurturing talent, fostering innovation, and upholding the democratic values that will shape the future of Ukraine.

In these dark times, our vision of a new, global university is not just a dream but a beacon of hope for us and for the generations to come.

This monograph focuses on the critical value of teaching IR during times of war. While my contribution may not emphasize IR extensively, I must highlight that, in my experience, political science and IR have become profoundly significant in such contexts. Before the war, Ukraine received limited attention in international scholarship, which allowed propaganda, skepticism, false narratives, and pop culture to dominate and influence international organizations. Many mistakes could have been avoided, and many lives could have been saved if more attention had been paid to high-quality, data-driven knowledge about Ukraine.

Another crucial lesson is that Ukraine had not sufficiently invested in its own scientific agency and representation prior to the invasion. Consequently, we had to invest in public activities, special issues, and the hiring of new faculty during the war — an endeavor that was both challenging and resource-intensive. Nevertheless, this investment was essential. We succeeded in promoting and hiring several strong political scholars in Ukraine, establishing KSE as a leading institution with five PONARS members (including full-time scholars and one academic board adviser). We edited two special issues and published them in *Foreign Affairs* specifically to raise awareness and build the capacity of Ukrainian scholars. Topics of IR have become embedded in our research and teaching activities; even the KSE Graduate Business School launched a new International Executive MBA with classes on geopolitics and IR. Despite our limited resources, we practiced what we preached by heavily investing in political science and IR. I hope this experience will be valuable to others who may still doubt the importance of IR.

References

Alexseev, M. A., & Dembitskyi, S. (2024a). For Victory in Freedom: Why Ukrainian Resilience to Russian Aggression Endures. *PONARS Eurasia*. https://www.ponarseurasia.org/for-victory-in-freedom-why-ukrainian-resilience-to-russian-aggression-endures/

Alexseev, M. A., & Dembitskyi, S. (2024b). Striking Back at the Empire: Ukrainians Converge on Values and National Belonging. *PONARS Eurasia.* https://www.ponarseurasia.org/striking-back-at-the-empire-ukrainians-converge-on-values-and-national-belonging/

Brik, T., Mylovanov, T., Murtazashvili, J. B., & Murtazashvili, I. (2024). Introduction: Special Issue on the Political Economy of the War in Ukraine. *Journal of Public Finance and Public Choice, 39*(1), 2-9.

De Rassenfosse, G., Murovana, T., & Uhlbach, W.-H. (2023). The Effects of War on Ukrainian Research. *Humanities and Social Sciences Communications, 10*(1), 1-11. https://www.nature.com/articles/s41599-023-02346-x

Ganguli, Ina, and Fabian Waldinger. "War and Science in Ukraine." *Entrepreneurship and Innovation Policy and the Economy* 3, no. 1 (2024): 165-188.

KSE Institute. (2024). *$155 Billion: The Total Amount of Damages Caused to Ukraine's Infrastructure Due to the War as of January 2024.* https://kse.ua/about-the-school/news/155-billion-the-total-amount-of-damages-caused-to-ukraine-s-infrastructure-due-to-the-war-as-of-january-2024/

KSE Institute. (2024). *Damages Report.* https://kse.ua/wp-content/uploads/2024/05/Eng_01.01.24_Damages_Report.pdf

KSE Institute (2025). The Russian Psychological Society After 2022: Serving the State, Shaping Ideology, Weaponizing Science. https://sanctions.kse.ua/en/the-russian-psychological-society-after-2022-serving-the-state-shaping-ideology-weaponizing-science/

Rabinovych, M., Brik, T., Darkovich, A., Savisko, M., Hatsko, V., Tytiuk, S., & Piddubnyi, I. (2023). Explaining Ukraine's Resilience to Russia's Invasion: The Role of Local Governance. *Governance.*

UNESCO. 2024. *Analysis of War Damage to the Ukrainian Science Sector and Its Consequences.* Paris: UNESCO.

About the Authors
(in Alphabetical Order)

Tymofii Brik is the rector at the Kyiv School of Economics and National Coordinator of the European Social Survey in Ukraine. He received his PhD in social science from Carlos III of Madrid and his MSc in sociology from Utrecht University and Kyiv Taras Shevchenko National University. Between 2018 and 2023, he had visiting positions at Northwestern, Stanford, and NYU universities. His papers appeared in *Governance, Journal of Comparative Economics*, and *Problems of Post-Communism*. His paper "When church competition matters?" published in the *Sociology of Religion*, won the N. Panina award in 2018 from the Institute of Sociology of the National Academy of Science of Ukraine.

Dr **Thomas Fetzer** is an Associate Professor at Central European University Vienna, Department of International Relations. His current research deals with the role of ideas in the IPE, with a specific focus on (economic) nationalism, as well as the relationship between IPE and security studies. Moreover, he is also involved in projects addressing the significance of history and memory politics for International Relations, with particular emphasis on the recent transformations unleashed by the Russo-Ukrainian war.

Dr **Olena Khylko** works as a Researcher at the Institute of European Studies and IR, Faculty of Social and Economic Sciences, at Comenius University in Bratislava. Previously, she worked as an Associate Professor at the Institute of International Relations, Taras Shevchenko National University of Kyiv. Along with academic experience, she contributed to the work of the think tanks, serving as the Director for Ukraine and Eastern Europe at Bratislava-based GLOBSEC and as the Expert at Kyiv-based East European Security

Research Initiative. Her research interests include but are not limited to Eastern European politics and security, postcoloniality, IR and geopolitics in the region and globally.

Ian Manners is a Professor in the Department of Political Science at Lund University and has previously worked at the University of Copenhagen, Roskilde University, Danish Institute for International Studies, Malmö University, University of Kent, Swansea University, and University of Bristol. His research is on the EU's normative power in planetary politics, examining the symbioses between planetary society, economy, ecology, conflict, and polity. His learning and teaching use research to inform courses on the Masters in European Affairs, international relations, and research methods, including the courses European Governance, Europe in Global Affairs, Everyday Europe, International Relations, and Political Cinema. His current research is focused on understanding the EU in planetary politics, including projects marking the twentieth anniversary of the normative power approach, such as a special issue entitled "Normative Power in the Planetary Organic Crisis" in *Cooperation and Conflict* and a forum, "Arrival of Normative Power in Planetary Politics" for the *Journal of Common Market Studies*.

Galyna Solovei is an Associate Professor of the Department of International Relations of the National University Kyiv-Mohyla Academy, was a visiting professor at the University of Amsterdam and the University of Carlos 3 in Madrid, and teaches a course on International Security at the University of Comillas, Madrid. She was part of projects to implement courses in violent conflict analysis in the curricula of the Kyiv-Mohyla Academy (2020-2023) and an academic adviser to the Model United Nations Club (2020-2023). She is currently participating in the research project "Challenges and Opportunities for EU Heritage Diplomacy in Ukraine."

About the Editors

Dr **Kateryna Zarembo** studied English and Italian as well as European politics and international relations at Kyiv and Dublin. She is an Associate Fellow of the New Europe Center, a member of PEN Ukraine, and has taught at the National University of Kyiv-Mohyla Academy, the Technical University of Darmstadt as well as the Central European University in Vienna. Her articles have appeared in, among other outlets, *European Societies*, *Problems of Post-Communism*, *European Security*, and the *Kyiv-Mohyla Law and Politics Journal*.

Dr **Michèle Knodt** studied political science at TU Darmstadt and did her PhD as well as Habilitation in Political Science at the University of Mannheim. She is a Professor of Political Science, Jean Monnet Chair (ad personam) and Director of the Jean Monnet Centre of Excellence EU in Global Dialogue (CEDI), Director of the Jean Monnet Centre of Excellence 'EU@School,' leader of the COST Action 17119 EU Foreign Policy facing new Realities (ENTER), Co-leader of the LOEWE Centre of Excellence 'emergenCITY,' and Co-leader of the DFG Research Training Group Critical Infrastructures. She serves as Research Area Leader of the Cluster Project 'Clean Circles' and Research Area Leader in the Kopernikus Project Ariadne—Evidence-Based Assessment for the Design of the German Energy System Transformation and is a leader of smaller cooperative and interdisciplinary projects. She has published widely on EU multi-level governance, is especially interested in resilience and emergency topics as well as energy and climate governance and has received research grants from the German Federal Ministry of Education and Research (BMBF), German Federal Ministry of Economic Affairs and Energy (BMWi), the German Research Council (DFG), the Volkswagen Foundation and the European Commission.

Dr **Maksym Yakovlyev** studied social work and comparative political science at the National University of Kyiv-Mohyla Academy (NaUKMA, Ukraine). He is the head of the International Relations Department at the National University of Kyiv-Mohyla Academy (NaUKMA) and the Director of the School for Policy Analysis at NaUKMA, a Kyiv-based university-affiliated think tank. For almost 11 years, he coordinated the double diploma MA project "German and European Studies" between the Friedrich Schiller University in Jena (Germany) and NaUKMA. He has published widely on research methodology, epistemology, and political concepts, and he frequently comments on international affairs for the Ukrainian and international media. Maksym Yakovlyev is also a member of the Public Council at Ukraine's Ministry of Foreign Affairs.

SOVIET AND POST-SOVIET POLITICS AND SOCIETY
Edited by Dr. Andreas Umland | ISSN 1614-3515

1. *Андреас Умланд (ред.)* | Воплощение Европейской конвенции по правам человека в России. Философские, юридические и эмпирические исследования | ISBN 3-89821-387-0

2. *Christian Wipperfürth* | Russland – ein vertrauenswürdiger Partner? Grundlagen, Hintergründe und Praxis gegenwärtiger russischer Außenpolitik | Mit einem Vorwort von Heinz Timmermann | ISBN 3-89821-401-X

3. *Manja Hussner* | Die Übernahme internationalen Rechts in die russische und deutsche Rechtsordnung. Eine vergleichende Analyse zur Völkerrechtsfreundlichkeit der Verfassungen der Russländischen Föderation und der Bundesrepublik Deutschland | Mit einem Vorwort von Rainer Arnold | ISBN 3-89821-438-9

4. *Matthew Tejada* | Bulgaria's Democratic Consolidation and the Kozloduy Nuclear Power Plant (KNPP). The Unattainability of Closure | With a foreword by Richard J. Crampton | ISBN 3-89821-439-7

5. *Марк Григорьевич Меерович* | Квадратные метры, определяющие сознание. Государственная жилищная политика в СССР. 1921 – 1941 гг | ISBN 3-89821-474-5

6. *Andrei P. Tsygankov, Pavel A.Tsygankov (Eds.)* | New Directions in Russian International Studies | ISBN 3-89821-422-2

7. *Марк Григорьевич Меерович* | Как власть народ к труду приучала. Жилище в СССР – средство управления людьми. 1917 – 1941 гг. | С предисловием Елены Осокиной | ISBN 3-89821-495-8

8. *David J. Galbreath* | Nation-Building and Minority Politics in Post-Socialist States. Interests, Influence and Identities in Estonia and Latvia | With a foreword by David J. Smith | ISBN 3-89821-467-2

9. *Алексей Юрьевич Безугольный* | Народы Кавказа в Вооружённых силах СССР в годы Великой Отечественной войны 1941-1945 гг. | С предисловием Николая Бугая | ISBN 3-89821-475-3

10. *Вячеслав Лихачев и Владимир Прибыловский (ред.)* | Русское Национальное Единство, 1990-2000. В 2-х томах | ISBN 3-89821-523-7

11. *Николай Бугай (ред.)* | Народы стран Балтии в условиях сталинизма (1940-е – 1950-е годы). Документированная история | ISBN 3-89821-525-1

12. *Ingmar Bredies (Hrsg.)* | Zur Anatomie der Orange Revolution in der Ukraine. Wechsel des Elitenregimes oder Triumph des Parlamentarismus? | ISBN 3-89821-524-5

13. *Anastasia V. Mitrofanova* | The Politicization of Russian Orthodoxy. Actors and Ideas | With a foreword by William C. Gay | ISBN 3-89821-481-8

14. *Nathan D. Larson* | Alexander Solzhenitsyn and the Russo-Jewish Question | ISBN 3-89821-483-4

15. *Guido Houben* | Kulturpolitik und Ethnizität. Staatliche Kunstförderung im Russland der neunziger Jahre | Mit einem Vorwort von Gert Weisskirchen | ISBN 3-89821-542-3

16. *Leonid Luks* | Der russische „Sonderweg"? Aufsätze zur neuesten Geschichte Russlands im europäischen Kontext | ISBN 3-89821-496-6

17. *Евгений Мороз* | История «Мёртвой воды» – от страшной сказки к большой политике. Политическое неоязычество в постсоветской России | ISBN 3-89821-551-2

18. *Александр Верховский и Галина Кожевникова (ред.)* | Этническая и религиозная интолерантность в российских СМИ. Результаты мониторинга 2001-2004 гг. | ISBN 3-89821-569-5

19. *Christian Ganzer* | Sowjetisches Erbe und ukrainische Nation. Das Museum der Geschichte des Zaporoger Kosakentums auf der Insel Chortycja | Mit einem Vorwort von Frank Golczewski | ISBN 3-89821-504-0

20. *Эльза-Баир Гучинова* | Помнить нельзя забыть. Антропология депортационной травмы калмыков | С предисловием Кэролайн Хамфри | ISBN 3-89821-506-7

21. *Юлия Лидерман* | Мотивы «проверки» и «испытания» в постсоветской культуре. Советское прошлое в российском кинематографе 1990-х годов | С предисловием Евгения Марголита | ISBN 3-89821-511-3

22. *Tanya Lokshina, Ray Thomas, Mary Mayer (Eds.)* | The Imposition of a Fake Political Settlement in the Northern Caucasus. The 2003 Chechen Presidential Election | ISBN 3-89821-436-2

23. *Timothy McCajor Hall, Rosie Read (Eds.)* | Changes in the Heart of Europe. Recent Ethnographies of Czechs, Slovaks, Roma, and Sorbs | With an afterword by Zdeněk Salzmann | ISBN 3-89821-606-3

24 *Christian Autengruber* | Die politischen Parteien in Bulgarien und Rumänien. Eine vergleichende Analyse seit Beginn der 90er Jahre | Mit einem Vorwort von Dorothée de Nève | ISBN 3-89821-476-1

25 *Annette Freyberg-Inan with Radu Cristescu* | The Ghosts in Our Classrooms, or: John Dewey Meets Ceauşescu. The Promise and the Failures of Civic Education in Romania | ISBN 3-89821-416-8

26 *John B. Dunlop* | The 2002 Dubrovka and 2004 Beslan Hostage Crises. A Critique of Russian Counter-Terrorism | With a foreword by Donald N. Jensen | ISBN 3-89821-608-X

27 *Peter Koller* | Das touristische Potenzial von Kam''janec'–Podil's'kyj. Eine fremdenverkehrsgeographische Untersuchung der Zukunftsperspektiven und Maßnahmenplanung zur Destinationsentwicklung des „ukrainischen Rothenburg" | Mit einem Vorwort von Kristiane Klemm | ISBN 3-89821-640-2

28 *Françoise Daucé, Elisabeth Sieca-Kozlowski (Eds.)* | Dedovshchina in the Post-Soviet Military. Hazing of Russian Army Conscripts in a Comparative Perspective | With a foreword by Dale Herspring | ISBN 3-89821-616-0

29 *Florian Strasser* | Zivilgesellschaftliche Einflüsse auf die Orange Revolution. Die gewaltlose Massenbewegung und die ukrainische Wahlkrise 2004 | Mit einem Vorwort von Egbert Jahn | ISBN 3-89821-648-9

30 *Rebecca S. Katz* | The Georgian Regime Crisis of 2003-2004. A Case Study in Post-Soviet Media Representation of Politics, Crime and Corruption | ISBN 3-89821-413-3

31 *Vladimir Kantor* | Willkür oder Freiheit. Beiträge zur russischen Geschichtsphilosophie | Ediert von Dagmar Herrmann sowie mit einem Vorwort versehen von Leonid Luks | ISBN 3-89821-589-X

32 *Laura A. Victoir* | The Russian Land Estate Today. A Case Study of Cultural Politics in Post-Soviet Russia | With a foreword by Priscilla Roosevelt | ISBN 3-89821-426-5

33 *Ivan Katchanovski* | Cleft Countries. Regional Political Divisions and Cultures in Post-Soviet Ukraine and Moldova | With a foreword by Francis Fukuyama | ISBN 3-89821-558-X

34 *Florian Mühlfried* | Postsowjetische Feiern. Das Georgische Bankett im Wandel | Mit einem Vorwort von Kevin Tuite | ISBN 3-89821-601-2

35 *Roger Griffin, Werner Loh, Andreas Umland (Eds.)* | Fascism Past and Present, West and East. An International Debate on Concepts and Cases in the Comparative Study of the Extreme Right | With an afterword by Walter Laqueur | ISBN 3-89821-674-8

36 *Sebastian Schlegel* | Der „Weiße Archipel". Sowjetische Atomstädte 1945-1991 | Mit einem Geleitwort von Thomas Bohn | ISBN 3-89821-679-9

37 *Vyacheslav Likhachev* | Political Anti-Semitism in Post-Soviet Russia. Actors and Ideas in 1991-2003 | Edited and translated from Russian by Eugene Veklerov | ISBN 3-89821-529-6

38 *Josette Baer (Ed.)* | Preparing Liberty in Central Europe. Political Texts from the Spring of Nations 1848 to the Spring of Prague 1968 | With a foreword by Zdeněk V. David | ISBN 3-89821-546-6

39 *Михаил Лукьянов* | Российский консерватизм и реформа, 1907-1914 | С предисловием Марка Д. Стейнберга | ISBN 3-89821-503-2

40 *Nicola Melloni* | Market Without Economy. The 1998 Russian Financial Crisis | With a foreword by Eiji Furukawa | ISBN 3-89821-407-9

41 *Dmitrij Chmelnizki* | Die Architektur Stalins | Bd. 1: Studien zu Ideologie und Stil | Bd. 2: Bilddokumentation | Mit einem Vorwort von Bruno Flierl | ISBN 3-89821-515-6

42 *Katja Yafimava* | Post-Soviet Russian-Belarussian Relationships. The Role of Gas Transit Pipelines | With a foreword by Jonathan P. Stern | ISBN 3-89821-655-1

43 *Boris Chavkin* | Verflechtungen der deutschen und russischen Zeitgeschichte. Aufsätze und Archivfunde zu den Beziehungen Deutschlands und der Sowjetunion von 1917 bis 1991 | Ediert von Markus Edlinger sowie mit einem Vorwort versehen von Leonid Luks | ISBN 3-89821-756-6

44 *Anastasija Grynenko in Zusammenarbeit mit Claudia Dathe* | Die Terminologie des Gerichtswesens der Ukraine und Deutschlands im Vergleich. Eine übersetzungswissenschaftliche Analyse juristischer Fachbegriffe im Deutschen, Ukrainischen und Russischen | Mit einem Vorwort von Ulrich Hartmann | ISBN 3-89821-691-8

45 *Anton Burkov* | The Impact of the European Convention on Human Rights on Russian Law. Legislation and Application in 1996-2006 | With a foreword by Françoise Hampson | ISBN 978-3-89821-639-5

46 *Stina Torjesen, Indra Overland (Eds.)* | International Election Observers in Post-Soviet Azerbaijan. Geopolitical Pawns or Agents of Change? | ISBN 978-3-89821-743-9

47 *Taras Kuzio* | Ukraine – Crimea – Russia. Triangle of Conflict | ISBN 978-3-89821-761-3

48 *Claudia Šabić* | „Ich erinnere mich nicht, aber L'viv!" Zur Funktion kultureller Faktoren für die Institutionalisierung und Entwicklung einer ukrainischen Region | Mit einem Vorwort von Melanie Tatur | ISBN 978-3-89821-752-1

49 *Marlies Bilz* | Tatarstan in der Transformation. Nationaler Diskurs und Politische Praxis 1988-1994 | Mit einem Vorwort von Frank Golczewski | ISBN 978-3-89821-722-4

50 *Марлен Ларюэль (ред.)* | Современные интерпретации русского национализма | ISBN 978-3-89821-795-8

51 *Sonja Schüler* | Die ethnische Dimension der Armut. Roma im postsozialistischen Rumänien | Mit einem Vorwort von Anton Sterbling | ISBN 978-3-89821-776-7

52 *Галина Кожевникова* | Радикальный национализм в России и противодействие ему. Сборник докладов Центра «Сова» за 2004-2007 гг. | С предисловием Александра Верховского | ISBN 978-3-89821-721-7

53 *Галина Кожевникова и Владимир Прибыловский* | Российская власть в биографиях I. Высшие должностные лица РФ в 2004 г. | ISBN 978-3-89821-796-5

54 *Галина Кожевникова и Владимир Прибыловский* | Российская власть в биографиях II. Члены Правительства РФ в 2004 г. | ISBN 978-3-89821-797-2

55 *Галина Кожевникова и Владимир Прибыловский* | Российская власть в биографиях III. Руководители федеральных служб и агентств РФ в 2004 г.| ISBN 978-3-89821-798-9

56 *Ileana Petroniu* | Privatisierung in Transformationsökonomien. Determinanten der Restrukturierungs-Bereitschaft am Beispiel Polens, Rumäniens und der Ukraine | Mit einem Vorwort von Rainer W. Schäfer | ISBN 978-3-89821-790-3

57 *Christian Wipperfürth* | Russland und seine GUS-Nachbarn. Hintergründe, aktuelle Entwicklungen und Konflikte in einer ressourcenreichen Region| ISBN 978-3-89821-801-6

58 *Togzhan Kassenova* | From Antagonism to Partnership. The Uneasy Path of the U.S.-Russian Cooperative Threat Reduction | With a foreword by Christoph Bluth | ISBN 978-3-89821-707-1

59 *Alexander Höllwerth* | Das sakrale eurasische Imperium des Aleksandr Dugin. Eine Diskursanalyse zum postsowjetischen russischen Rechtsextremismus | Mit einem Vorwort von Dirk Uffelmann | ISBN 978-3-89821-813-9

60 *Олег Рябов* | «Россия-Матушка». Национализм, гендер и война в России XX века | С предисловием Елены Гощило | ISBN 978-3-89821-487-2

61 *Ivan Maistrenko* | Borot'bism. A Chapter in the History of the Ukrainian Revolution | With a new Introduction by Chris Ford | Translated by George S. N. Luckyj with the assistance of Ivan L. Rudnytsky | Second, Revised and Expanded Edition ISBN 978-3-8382-1107-7

62 *Maryna Romanets* | Anamorphosic Texts and Reconfigured Visions. Improvised Traditions in Contemporary Ukrainian and Irish Literature | ISBN 978-3-89821-576-3

63 *Paul D'Anieri and Taras Kuzio (Eds.)* | Aspects of the Orange Revolution I. Democratization and Elections in Post-Communist Ukraine | ISBN 978-3-89821-698-2

64 *Bohdan Harasymiw in collaboration with Oleh S. Ilnytzkyj (Eds.)* | Aspects of the Orange Revolution II. Information and Manipulation Strategies in the 2004 Ukrainian Presidential Elections | ISBN 978-3-89821-699-9

65 *Ingmar Bredies, Andreas Umland and Valentin Yakushik (Eds.)* | Aspects of the Orange Revolution III. The Context and Dynamics of the 2004 Ukrainian Presidential Elections | ISBN 978-3-89821-803-0

66 *Ingmar Bredies, Andreas Umland and Valentin Yakushik (Eds.)* | Aspects of the Orange Revolution IV. Foreign Assistance and Civic Action in the 2004 Ukrainian Presidential Elections | ISBN 978-3-89821-808-5

67 *Ingmar Bredies, Andreas Umland and Valentin Yakushik (Eds.)* | Aspects of the Orange Revolution V. Institutional Observation Reports on the 2004 Ukrainian Presidential Elections | ISBN 978-3-89821-809-2

68 *Taras Kuzio (Ed.)* | Aspects of the Orange Revolution VI. Post-Communist Democratic Revolutions in Comparative Perspective | ISBN 978-3-89821-820-7

69 *Tim Bohse* | Autoritarismus statt Selbstverwaltung. Die Transformation der kommunalen Politik in der Stadt Kaliningrad 1990-2005 | Mit einem Geleitwort von Stefan Troebst | ISBN 978-3-89821-782-8

70 *David Rupp* | Die Rußländische Föderation und die russischsprachige Minderheit in Lettland. Eine Fallstudie zur Anwaltspolitik Moskaus gegenüber den russophonen Minderheiten im „Nahen Ausland" von 1991 bis 2002 | Mit einem Vorwort von Helmut Wagner | ISBN 978-3-89821-778-1

71 *Taras Kuzio* | Theoretical and Comparative Perspectives on Nationalism. New Directions in Cross-Cultural and Post-Communist Studies | With a foreword by Paul Robert Magocsi | ISBN 978-3-89821-815-3

72 *Christine Teichmann* | Die Hochschultransformation im heutigen Osteuropa. Kontinuität und Wandel bei der Entwicklung des postkommunistischen Universitätswesens | Mit einem Vorwort von Oskar Anweiler | ISBN 978-3-89821-842-9

73 *Julia Kusznir* | Der politische Einfluss von Wirtschaftseliten in russischen Regionen. Eine Analyse am Beispiel der Erdöl- und Erdgasindustrie, 1992-2005 | Mit einem Vorwort von Wolfgang Eichwede | ISBN 978-3-89821-821-4

74 *Alena Vysotskaya* | Russland, Belarus und die EU-Osterweiterung. Zur Minderheitenfrage und zum Problem der Freizügigkeit des Personenverkehrs | Mit einem Vorwort von Katlijn Malfliet | ISBN 978-3-89821-822-1

75 *Heiko Pleines (Hrsg.)* | Corporate Governance in post-sozialistischen Volkswirtschaften | ISBN 978-3-89821-766-8

76 *Stefan Ihrig* | Wer sind die Moldawier? Rumänismus versus Moldowanismus in Historiographie und Schulbüchern der Republik Moldova, 1991-2006 | Mit einem Vorwort von Holm Sundhaussen | ISBN 978-3-89821-466-7

77 *Galina Kozhevnikova in collaboration with Alexander Verkhovsky and Eugene Veklerov* | Ultra-Nationalism and Hate Crimes in Contemporary Russia. The 2004-2006 Annual Reports of Moscow's SOVA Center | With a foreword by Stephen D. Shenfield | ISBN 978-3-89821-868-9

78 *Florian Küchler* | The Role of the European Union in Moldova's Transnistria Conflict | With a foreword by Christopher Hill | ISBN 978-3-89821-850-4

79 *Bernd Rechel* | The Long Way Back to Europe. Minority Protection in Bulgaria | With a foreword by Richard Crampton | ISBN 978-3-89821-863-4

80 *Peter W. Rodgers* | Nation, Region and History in Post-Communist Transitions. Identity Politics in Ukraine, 1991-2006 | With a foreword by Vera Tolz | ISBN 978-3-89821-903-7

81 *Stephanie Solywoda* | The Life and Work of Semen L. Frank. A Study of Russian Religious Philosophy | With a foreword by Philip Walters | ISBN 978-3-89821-457-5

82 *Vera Sokolova* | Cultural Politics of Ethnicity. Discourses on Roma in Communist Czechoslovakia | ISBN 978-3-89821-864-1

83 *Natalya Shevchik Ketenci* | Kazakhstani Enterprises in Transition. The Role of Historical Regional Development in Kazakhstan's Post-Soviet Economic Transformation | ISBN 978-3-89821-831-3

84 *Martin Malek, Anna Schor-Tschudnowskaja (Hgg.)* | Europa im Tschetschenienkrieg. Zwischen politischer Ohnmacht und Gleichgültigkeit | Mit einem Vorwort von Lipchan Basajewa | ISBN 978-3-89821-676-0

85 *Stefan Meister* | Das postsowjetische Universitätswesen zwischen nationalem und internationalem Wandel. Die Entwicklung der regionalen Hochschule in Russland als Gradmesser der Systemtransformation | Mit einem Vorwort von Joan DeBardeleben | ISBN 978-3-89821-891-7

86 *Konstantin Sheiko in collaboration with Stephen Brown* | Nationalist Imaginings of the Russian Past. Anatolii Fomenko and the Rise of Alternative History in Post-Communist Russia | With a foreword by Donald Ostrowski | ISBN 978-3-89821-915-0

87 *Sabine Jenni* | Wie stark ist das „Einige Russland"? Zur Parteibindung der Eliten und zum Wahlerfolg der Machtpartei im Dezember 2007 | Mit einem Vorwort von Klaus Armingeon | ISBN 978-3-89821-961-7

88 *Thomas Borén* | Meeting-Places of Transformation. Urban Identity, Spatial Representations and Local Politics in Post-Soviet St Petersburg | ISBN 978-3-89821-739-2

89 *Aygul Ashirova* | Stalinismus und Stalin-Kult in Zentralasien. Turkmenistan 1924-1953 | Mit einem Vorwort von Leonid Luks | ISBN 978-3-89821-987-7

90 *Leonid Luks* | Freiheit oder imperiale Größe? Essays zu einem russischen Dilemma | ISBN 978-3-8382-0011-8

91 *Christopher Gilley* | The 'Change of Signposts' in the Ukrainian Emigration. A Contribution to the History of Sovietophilism in the 1920s | With a foreword by Frank Golczewski | ISBN 978-3-89821-965-5

92 *Philipp Casula, Jeronim Perovic (Eds.)* | Identities and Politics During the Putin Presidency. The Discursive Foundations of Russia's Stability | With a foreword by Heiko Haumann | ISBN 978-3-8382-0015-6

93 *Marcel Viëtor* | Europa und die Frage nach seinen Grenzen im Osten. Zur Konstruktion ‚europäischer Identität' in Geschichte und Gegenwart | Mit einem Vorwort von Albrecht Lehmann | ISBN 978-3-8382-0045-3

94 *Ben Hellman, Andrei Rogachevskii* | Filming the Unfilmable. Casper Wrede's 'One Day in the Life of Ivan Denisovich' | Second, Revised and Expanded Edition | ISBN 978-3-8382-0044-6

95 *Eva Fuchslocher* | Vaterland, Sprache, Glaube. Orthodoxie und Nationenbildung am Beispiel Georgiens | Mit einem Vorwort von Christina von Braun | ISBN 978-3-89821-884-9

96 *Vladimir Kantor* | Das Westlertum und der Weg Russlands. Zur Entwicklung der russischen Literatur und Philosophie | Ediert von Dagmar Herrmann | Mit einem Beitrag von Nikolaus Lobkowicz | ISBN 978-3-8382-0102-3

97 *Kamran Musayev* | Die postsowjetische Transformation im Baltikum und Südkaukasus. Eine vergleichende Untersuchung der politischen Entwicklung Lettlands und Aserbaidschans 1985-2009 | Mit einem Vorwort von Leonid Luks | Ediert von Sandro Henschel | ISBN 978-3-8382-0103-0

98 *Tatiana Zhurzhenko* | Borderlands into Bordered Lands. Geopolitics of Identity in Post-Soviet Ukraine | With a foreword by Dieter Segert | ISBN 978-3-8382-0042-2

99 *Кирилл Галушко, Лидия Смола (ред.)* | Пределы падения – варианты украинского будущего. Аналитико-прогностические исследования | ISBN 978-3-8382-0148-1

100 *Michael Minkenberg (Ed.)* | Historical Legacies and the Radical Right in Post-Cold War Central and Eastern Europe | With an afterword by Sabrina P. Ramet | ISBN 978-3-8382-0124-5

101 *David-Emil Wickström* | Rocking St. Petersburg. Transcultural Flows and Identity Politics in the St. Petersburg Popular Music Scene | With a foreword by Yngvar B. Steinholt | Second, Revised and Expanded Edition | ISBN 978-3-8382-0100-9

102 *Eva Zabka* | Eine neue „Zeit der Wirren"? Der spät- und postsowjetische Systemwandel 1985-2000 im Spiegel russischer gesellschaftspolitischer Diskurse | Mit einem Vorwort von Margareta Mommsen | ISBN 978-3-8382-0161-0

103 *Ulrike Ziemer* | Ethnic Belonging, Gender and Cultural Practices. Youth Identitites in Contemporary Russia | With a foreword by Anoop Nayak | ISBN 978-3-8382-0152-8

104 *Ksenia Chepikova* | ‚Einiges Russland' - eine zweite KPdSU? Aspekte der Identitätskonstruktion einer postsowjetischen „Partei der Macht" | Mit einem Vorwort von Torsten Oppelland | ISBN 978-3-8382-0311-9

105 *Леонид Люкс* | Западничество или евразийство? Демократия или идеократия? Сборник статей об исторических дилеммах России | С предисловием Владимира Кантора | ISBN 978-3-8382-0211-2

106 *Anna Dost* | Das russische Verfassungsrecht auf dem Weg zum Föderalismus und zurück. Zum Konflikt von Rechtsnormen und -wirklichkeit in der Russländischen Föderation von 1991 bis 2009 | Mit einem Vorwort von Alexander Blankenagel | ISBN 978-3-8382-0292-1

107 *Philipp Herzog* | Sozialistische Völkerfreundschaft, nationaler Widerstand oder harmloser Zeitvertreib? Zur politischen Funktion der Volkskunst im sowjetischen Estland | Mit einem Vorwort von Andreas Kappeler | ISBN 978-3-8382-0216-7

108 *Marlène Laruelle (Ed.)* | Russian Nationalism, Foreign Policy, and Identity Debates in Putin's Russia. New Ideological Patterns after the Orange Revolution | ISBN 978-3-8382-0325-6

109 *Michail Logvinov* | Russlands Kampf gegen den internationalen Terrorismus. Eine kritische Bestandsaufnahme des Bekämpfungsansatzes | Mit einem Geleitwort von Hans-Henning Schröder und einem Vorwort von Eckhard Jesse | ISBN 978-3-8382-0329-4

110 *John B. Dunlop* | The Moscow Bombings of September 1999. Examinations of Russian Terrorist Attacks at the Onset of Vladimir Putin's Rule | Second, Revised and Expanded Edition | ISBN 978-3-8382-0388-1

111 *Андрей А. Ковалёв* | Свидетельство из-за кулис российской политики I. Можно ли делать добро из зла? (Воспоминания и размышления о последних советских и первых послесоветских годах) | With a foreword by Peter Reddaway | ISBN 978-3-8382-0302-7

112 *Андрей А. Ковалёв* | Свидетельство из-за кулис российской политики II. Угроза для себя и окружающих (Наблюдения и предостережения относительно происходящего после 2000 г.) | ISBN 978-3-8382-0303-4

113 *Bernd Kappenberg* | Zeichen setzen für Europa. Der Gebrauch europäischer lateinischer Sonderzeichen in der deutschen Öffentlichkeit | Mit einem Vorwort von Peter Schlobinski | ISBN 978-3-89821-749-1

114 *Ivo Mijnssen* | The Quest for an Ideal Youth in Putin's Russia I. Back to Our Future! History, Modernity, and Patriotism according to Nashi, 2005-2013 | With a foreword by Jeronim Perović | Second, Revised and Expanded Edition | ISBN 978-3-8382-0368-3

115 *Jussi Lassila* | The Quest for an Ideal Youth in Putin's Russia II. The Search for Distinctive Conformism in the Political Communication of Nashi, 2005-2009 | With a foreword by Kirill Postoutenko | Second, Revised and Expanded Edition | ISBN 978-3-8382-0415-4

116 *Valerio Trabandt* | Neue Nachbarn, gute Nachbarschaft? Die EU als internationaler Akteur am Beispiel ihrer Demokratieförderung in Belarus und der Ukraine 2004-2009 | Mit einem Vorwort von Jutta Joachim | ISBN 978-3-8382-0437-6

117 *Fabian Pfeiffer* | Estlands Außen- und Sicherheitspolitik I. Der estnische Atlantizismus nach der wiedererlangten Unabhängigkeit 1991-2004 | Mit einem Vorwort von Helmut Hubel | ISBN 978-3-8382-0127-6

118 *Jana Podßuweit* | Estlands Außen- und Sicherheitspolitik II. Handlungsoptionen eines Kleinstaates im Rahmen seiner EU-Mitgliedschaft (2004-2008) | Mit einem Vorwort von Helmut Hubel | ISBN 978-3-8382-0440-6

119 *Karin Pointner* | Estlands Außen- und Sicherheitspolitik III. Eine gedächtnispolitische Analyse estnischer Entwicklungskooperation 2006-2010 | Mit einem Vorwort von Karin Liebhart | ISBN 978-3-8382-0435-2

120 *Ruslana Vovk* | Die Offenheit der ukrainischen Verfassung für das Völkerrecht und die europäische Integration | Mit einem Vorwort von Alexander Blankenagel | ISBN 978-3-8382-0481-9

121 *Mykhaylo Banakh* | Die Relevanz der Zivilgesellschaft bei den postkommunistischen Transformationsprozessen in mittel- und osteuropäischen Ländern. Das Beispiel der spät- und postsowjetischen Ukraine 1986-2009 | Mit einem Vorwort von Gerhard Simon | ISBN 978-3-8382-0499-4

122 *Michael Moser* | Language Policy and the Discourse on Languages in Ukraine under President Viktor Yanukovych (25 February 2010–28 October 2012) | ISBN 978-3-8382-0497-0 (Paperback edition) | ISBN 978-3-8382-0507-6 (Hardcover edition)

123 *Nicole Krome* | Russischer Netzwerkkapitalismus Restrukturierungsprozesse in der Russischen Föderation am Beispiel des Luftfahrtunternehmens „Aviastar" | Mit einem Vorwort von Petra Stykow | ISBN 978-3-8382-0534-2

124 *David R. Marples* | 'Our Glorious Past'. Lukashenka's Belarus and the Great Patriotic War | ISBN 978-3-8382-0574-8 (Paperback edition) | ISBN 978-3-8382-0675-2 (Hardcover edition)

125 *Ulf Walther* | Russlands „neuer Adel". Die Macht des Geheimdienstes von Gorbatschow bis Putin | Mit einem Vorwort von Hans-Georg Wieck | ISBN 978-3-8382-0584-7

126 *Simon Geissbühler (Hrsg.)* | Kiew – Revolution 3.0. Der Euromaidan 2013/14 und die Zukunftsperspektiven der Ukraine | ISBN 978-3-8382-0581-6 (Paperback edition) | ISBN 978-3-8382-0681-3 (Hardcover edition)

127 *Andrey Makarychev* | Russia and the EU in a Multipolar World. Discourses, Identities, Norms | With a foreword by Klaus Segbers | ISBN 978-3-8382-0629-5

128 *Roland Scharff* | Kasachstan als postsowjetischer Wohlfahrtsstaat. Die Transformation des sozialen Schutzsystems | Mit einem Vorwort von Joachim Ahrens | ISBN 978-3-8382-0622-6

129 *Katja Grupp* | Bild Lücke Deutschland. Kaliningrader Studierende sprechen über Deutschland | Mit einem Vorwort von Martin Schulz | ISBN 978-3-8382-0552-6

130 *Konstantin Sheiko, Stephen Brown* | History as Therapy. Alternative History and Nationalist Imaginings in Russia, 1991-2014 | ISBN 978-3-8382-0665-3

131 *Elisa Kriza* | Alexander Solzhenitsyn: Cold War Icon, Gulag Author, Russian Nationalist? A Study of the Western Reception of his Literary Writings, Historical Interpretations, and Political Ideas | With a foreword by Andrei Rogatchevski | ISBN 978-3-8382-0589-2 (Paperback edition) | ISBN 978-3-8382-0690-5 (Hardcover edition)

132 *Serghei Golunov* | The Elephant in the Room. Corruption and Cheating in Russian Universities | ISBN 978-3-8382-0570-0

133 *Manja Hussner, Rainer Arnold (Hgg.)* | Verfassungsgerichtsbarkeit in Zentralasien I. Sammlung von Verfassungstexten | ISBN 978-3-8382-0595-3

134 *Nikolay Mitrokhin* | Die „Russische Partei". Die Bewegung der russischen Nationalisten in der UdSSR 1953-1985 | Aus dem Russischen übertragen von einem Übersetzerteam unter der Leitung von Larisa Schippel | ISBN 978-3-8382-0024-8

135 *Manja Hussner, Rainer Arnold (Hgg.)* | Verfassungsgerichtsbarkeit in Zentralasien II. Sammlung von Verfassungstexten | ISBN 978-3-8382-0597-7

136 *Manfred Zeller* | Das sowjetische Fieber. Fußballfans im poststalinistischen Vielvölkerreich | Mit einem Vorwort von Nikolaus Katzer | ISBN 978-3-8382-0757-5

137 *Kristin Schreiter* | Stellung und Entwicklungspotential zivilgesellschaftlicher Gruppen in Russland. Menschenrechtsorganisationen im Vergleich | ISBN 978-3-8382-0673-8

138 *David R. Marples, Frederick V. Mills (Eds.)* | Ukraine's Euromaidan. Analyses of a Civil Revolution | ISBN 978-3-8382-0660-8

139 *Bernd Kappenberg* | Setting Signs for Europe. Why Diacritics Matter for European Integration | With a foreword by Peter Schlobinski | ISBN 978-3-8382-0663-9

140 *René Lenz* | Internationalisierung, Kooperation und Transfer. Externe bildungspolitische Akteure in der Russischen Föderation | Mit einem Vorwort von Frank Ettrich | ISBN 978-3-8382-0751-3

141 *Juri Plusnin, Yana Zausaeva, Natalia Zhidkevich, Artemy Pozanenko* | Wandering Workers. Mores, Behavior, Way of Life, and Political Status of Domestic Russian Labor Migrants | Translated by Julia Kazantseva | ISBN 978-3-8382-0653-0

142 *David J. Smith (Eds.)* | Latvia – A Work in Progress? 100 Years of State- and Nation-Building | ISBN 978-3-8382-0648-6

143 *Инна Чувычкина (ред.)* | Экспортные нефте- и газопроводы на постсоветском пространстве. Анализ трубопроводной политики в свете теории международных отношений | ISBN 978-3-8382-0822-0

144 *Johann Zajaczkowski* | Russland – eine pragmatische Großmacht? Eine rollentheoretische Untersuchung russischer Außenpolitik am Beispiel der Zusammenarbeit mit den USA nach 9/11 und des Georgienkrieges von 2008 | Mit einem Vorwort von Siegfried Schieder | ISBN 978-3-8382-0837-4

145 *Boris Popivanov* | Changing Images of the Left in Bulgaria. The Challenge of Post-Communism in the Early 21st Century | ISBN 978-3-8382-0667-7

146 *Lenka Krátká* | A History of the Czechoslovak Ocean Shipping Company 1948-1989. How a Small, Landlocked Country Ran Maritime Business During the Cold War | ISBN 978-3-8382-0666-0

147 *Alexander Sergunin* | Explaining Russian Foreign Policy Behavior. Theory and Practice | ISBN 978-3-8382-0752-0

148 *Darya Malyutina* | Migrant Friendships in a Super-Diverse City. Russian-Speakers and their Social Relationships in London in the 21st Century | With a foreword by Claire Dwyer | ISBN 978-3-8382-0652-3

149 *Alexander Sergunin, Valery Konyshev* | Russia in the Arctic. Hard or Soft Power? | ISBN 978-3-8382-0753-7

150 *John J. Maresca* | Helsinki Revisited. A Key U.S. Negotiator's Memoirs on the Development of the CSCE into the OSCE | With a foreword by Hafiz Pashayev | ISBN 978-3-8382-0852-7

151 *Jardar Østbø* | The New Third Rome. Readings of a Russian Nationalist Myth | With a foreword by Pål Kolstø | ISBN 978-3-8382-0870-1

152 *Simon Kordonsky* | Socio-Economic Foundations of the Russian Post-Soviet Regime. The Resource-Based Economy and Estate-Based Social Structure of Contemporary Russia | With a foreword by Svetlana Barsukova | ISBN 978-3-8382-0775-9

153 *Duncan Leitch* | Assisting Reform in Post-Communist Ukraine 2000–2012. The Illusions of Donors and the Disillusion of Beneficiaries | With a foreword by Kataryna Wolczuk | ISBN 978-3-8382-0844-2

154 *Abel Polese* | Limits of a Post-Soviet State. How Informality Replaces, Renegotiates, and Reshapes Governance in Contemporary Ukraine | With a foreword by Colin Williams | ISBN 978-3-8382-0845-9

155 *Mikhail Suslov (Ed.)* | Digital Orthodoxy in the Post-Soviet World. The Russian Orthodox Church and Web 2.0 | With a foreword by Father Cyril Hovorun | ISBN 978-3-8382-0871-8

156 *Leonid Luks* | Zwei „Sonderwege"? Russisch-deutsche Parallelen und Kontraste (1917-2014). Vergleichende Essays | ISBN 978-3-8382-0823-7

157 *Vladimir V. Karacharovskiy, Ovsey I. Shkaratan, Gordey A. Yastrebov* | Towards a New Russian Work Culture. Can Western Companies and Expatriates Change Russian Society? | With a foreword by Elena N. Danilova | Translated by Julia Kazantseva | ISBN 978-3-8382-0902-9

158 *Edmund Griffiths* | Aleksandr Prokhanov and Post-Soviet Esotericism | ISBN 978-3-8382-0963-0

159 *Timm Beichelt, Susann Worschech (Eds.)* | Transnational Ukraine? Networks and Ties that Influence(d) Contemporary Ukraine | ISBN 978-3-8382-0944-9

160 *Mieste Hotopp-Riecke* | Die Tataren der Krim zwischen Assimilation und Selbstbehauptung. Der Aufbau des krimtatarischen Bildungswesens nach Deportation und Heimkehr (1990-2005) | Mit einem Vorwort von Swetlana Czerwonnaja | ISBN 978-3-89821-940-2

161 *Olga Bertelsen (Ed.)* | Revolution and War in Contemporary Ukraine. The Challenge of Change | ISBN 978-3-8382-1016-2

162 *Natalya Ryabinska* | Ukraine's Post-Communist Mass Media. Between Capture and Commercialization | With a foreword by Marta Dyczok | ISBN 978-3-8382-1011-7

163 *Alexandra Cotofana, James M. Nyce (Eds.)* | Religion and Magic in Socialist and Post-Socialist Contexts. Historic and Ethnographic Case Studies of Orthodoxy, Heterodoxy, and Alternative Spirituality | With a foreword by Patrick L. Michelson | ISBN 978-3-8382-0989-0

164 *Nozima Akhrarkhodjaeva* | The Instrumentalisation of Mass Media in Electoral Authoritarian Regimes. Evidence from Russia's Presidential Election Campaigns of 2000 and 2008 | ISBN 978-3-8382-1013-1

165 *Yulia Krasheninnikova* | Informal Healthcare in Contemporary Russia. Sociographic Essays on the Post-Soviet Infrastructure for Alternative Healing Practices | ISBN 978-3-8382-0970-8

166 *Peter Kaiser* | Das Schachbrett der Macht. Die Handlungsspielräume eines sowjetischen Funktionärs unter Stalin am Beispiel des Generalsekretärs des Komsomol Aleksandr Kosarev (1929-1938) | Mit einem Vorwort von Dietmar Neutatz | ISBN 978-3-8382-1052-0

167 *Oksana Kim* | The Effects and Implications of Kazakhstan's Adoption of International Financial Reporting Standards. A Resource Dependence Perspective | With a foreword by Svetlana Vlady | ISBN 978-3-8382-0987-6

168 *Anna Sanina* | Patriotic Education in Contemporary Russia. Sociological Studies in the Making of the Post-Soviet Citizen | With a foreword by Anna Oldfield | ISBN 978-3-8382-0993-7

169 *Rudolf Wolters* | Spezialist in Sibirien Faksimile der 1933 erschienenen ersten Ausgabe | Mit einem Vorwort von Dmitrij Chmelnizki | ISBN 978-3-8382-0515-1

170 *Michal Vít, Magdalena M. Baran (Eds.)* | Transregional versus National Perspectives on Contemporary Central European History. Studies on the Building of Nation-States and Their Cooperation in the 20th and 21st Century | With a foreword by Petr Vágner | ISBN 978-3-8382-1015-5

171 *Philip Gamaghelyan* | Conflict Resolution Beyond the International Relations Paradigm. Evolving Designs as a Transformative Practice in Nagorno-Karabakh and Syria | With a foreword by Susan Allen | ISBN 978-3-8382-1057-5

172 *Maria Shagina* | Joining a Prestigious Club. Cooperation with Europarties and Its Impact on Party Development in Georgia, Moldova, and Ukraine 2004–2015 | With a foreword by Kataryna Wolczuk | ISBN 978-3-8382-1084-1

173 *Alexandra Cotofana, James M. Nyce (Eds.)* | Religion and Magic in Socialist and Post-Socialist Contexts II. Baltic, Eastern European, and Post-USSR Case Studies | With a foreword by Anita Stasulane | ISBN 978-3-8382-0990-6

174 *Barbara Kunz* | Kind Words, Cruise Missiles, and Everything in Between. The Use of Power Resources in U.S. Policies towards Poland, Ukraine, and Belarus 1989–2008 | With a foreword by William Hill | ISBN 978-3-8382-1065-0

175 *Eduard Klein* | Bildungskorruption in Russland und der Ukraine. Eine komparative Analyse der Performanz staatlicher Antikorruptionsmaßnahmen im Hochschulsektor am Beispiel universitärer Aufnahmeprüfungen | Mit einem Vorwort von Heiko Pleines | ISBN 978-3-8382-0995-1

176 *Markus Soldner* | Politischer Kapitalismus im postsowjetischen Russland. Die politische, wirtschaftliche und mediale Transformation in den 1990er Jahren | Mit einem Vorwort von Wolfgang Ismayr | ISBN 978-3-8382-1222-7

177 *Anton Oleinik* | Building Ukraine from Within. A Sociological, Institutional, and Economic Analysis of a Nation-State in the Making | ISBN 978-3-8382-1150-3

178 *Peter Rollberg, Marlene Laruelle (Eds.)* | Mass Media in the Post-Soviet World. Market Forces, State Actors, and Political Manipulation in the Informational Environment after Communism | ISBN 978-3-8382-1116-9

179 *Mikhail Minakov* | Development and Dystopia. Studies in Post-Soviet Ukraine and Eastern Europe | With a foreword by Alexander Etkind | ISBN 978-3-8382-1112-1

180 *Aijan Sharshenova* | The European Union's Democracy Promotion in Central Asia. A Study of Political Interests, Influence, and Development in Kazakhstan and Kyrgyzstan in 2007–2013 | With a foreword by Gordon Crawford | ISBN 978-3-8382-1151-0

181 *Andrey Makarychev, Alexandra Yatsyk (Eds.)* | Boris Nemtsov and Russian Politics. Power and Resistance | With a foreword by Zhanna Nemtsova | ISBN 978-3-8382-1122-0

182 *Sophie Falsini* | The Euromaidan's Effect on Civil Society. Why and How Ukrainian Social Capital Increased after the Revolution of Dignity | With a foreword by Susann Worschech | ISBN 978-3-8382-1131-2

183 *Valentyna Romanova, Andreas Umland (Eds.)* | Ukraine's Decentralization. Challenges and Implications of the Local Governance Reform after the Euromaidan Revolution | ISBN 978-3-8382-1162-6

184 *Leonid Luks* | A Fateful Triangle. Essays on Contemporary Russian, German and Polish History | ISBN 978-3-8382-1143-5

185 *John B. Dunlop* | The February 2015 Assassination of Boris Nemtsov and the Flawed Trial of his Alleged Killers. An Exploration of Russia's "Crime of the 21st Century" | ISBN 978-3-8382-1188-6

186 *Vasile Rotaru* | Russia, the EU, and the Eastern Partnership. Building Bridges or Digging Trenches? | ISBN 978-3-8382-1134-3

187 *Marina Lebedeva* | Russian Studies of International Relations. From the Soviet Past to the Post-Cold-War Present | With a foreword by Andrei P. Tsygankov | ISBN 978-3-8382-0851-0

188 *Tomasz Stepniewski, George Soroka (Eds.)* | Ukraine after Maidan. Revisiting Domestic and Regional Security | ISBN 978-3-8382-1075-9

189 *Petar Cholakov* | Ethnic Entrepreneurs Unmasked. Political Institutions and Ethnic Conflicts in Contemporary Bulgaria | ISBN 978-3-8382-1189-3

190 *A. Salem, G. Hazeldine, D. Morgan (Eds.)* | Higher Education in Post-Communist States. Comparative and Sociological Perspectives | ISBN 978-3-8382-1183-1

191 *Igor Torbakov* | After Empire. Nationalist Imagination and Symbolic Politics in Russia and Eurasia in the Twentieth and Twenty-First Century | With a foreword by Serhii Plokhy | ISBN 978-3-8382-1217-3

192 *Aleksandr Burakovskiy* | Jewish-Ukrainian Relations in Late and Post-Soviet Ukraine. Articles, Lectures and Essays from 1986 to 2016 | ISBN 978-3-8382-1210-4

193 *Natalia Shapovalova, Olga Burlyuk (Eds.)* | Civil Society in Post-Euromaidan Ukraine. From Revolution to Consolidation | With a foreword by Richard Youngs | ISBN 978-3-8382-1216-6

194 *Franz Preissler* | Positionsverteidigung, Imperialismus oder Irredentismus? Russland und die „Russischsprachigen", 1991–2015 | ISBN 978-3-8382-1262-3

195 *Marian Madeła* | Der Reformprozess in der Ukraine 2014-2017. Eine Fallstudie zur Reform der öffentlichen Verwaltung | Mit einem Vorwort von Martin Malek | ISBN 978-3-8382-1266-1

196 *Anke Giesen* | „Wie kann denn der Sieger ein Verbrecher sein?" Eine diskursanalytische Untersuchung der russlandweiten Debatte über Konzept und Verstaatlichungsprozess der Lagergedenkstätte „Perm'-36" im Ural | ISBN 978-3-8382-1284-5

197 *Victoria Leukavets* | The Integration Policies of Belarus and Ukraine vis-à-vis the EU and Russia. A Comparative Analysis Through the Prism of a Two-Level Game Approach | ISBN 978-3-8382-1247-0

198 *Oksana Kim* | The Development and Challenges of Russian Corporate Governance I. The Roles and Functions of Boards of Directors | With a foreword by Sheila M. Puffer | ISBN 978-3-8382-1287-6

199 *Thomas D. Grant* | International Law and the Post-Soviet Space I. Essays on Chechnya and the Baltic States | With a foreword by Stephen M. Schwebel | ISBN 978-3-8382-1279-1

200 *Thomas D. Grant* | International Law and the Post-Soviet Space II. Essays on Ukraine, Intervention, and Non-Proliferation | ISBN 978-3-8382-1280-7

201 *Slavomír Michálek, Michal Štefansky* | The Age of Fear. The Cold War and Its Influence on Czechoslovakia 1945–1968 | ISBN 978-3-8382-1285-2

202 *Iulia-Sabina Joja* | Romania's Strategic Culture 1990–2014. Continuity and Change in a Post-Communist Country's Evolution of National Interests and Security Policies | With a foreword by Heiko Biehl | ISBN 978-3-8382-1286-9

203 *Andrei Rogatchevski, Yngvar B. Steinholt, Arve Hansen, David-Emil Wickström* | War of Songs. Popular Music and Recent Russia-Ukraine Relations | With a foreword by Artemy Troitsky | ISBN 978-3-8382-1173-2

204 *Maria Lipman (Ed.)* | Russian Voices on Post-Crimea Russia. An Almanac of Counterpoint Essays from 2015–2018 | ISBN 978-3-8382-1251-7

205 *Ksenia Maksimovtsova* | Language Conflicts in Contemporary Estonia, Latvia, and Ukraine. A Comparative Exploration of Discourses in Post-Soviet Russian-Language Digital Media | With a foreword by Ammon Cheskin | ISBN 978-3-8382-1282-1

206 *Michal Vít* | The EU's Impact on Identity Formation in East-Central Europe between 2004 and 2013. Perceptions of the Nation and Europe in Political Parties of the Czech Republic, Poland, and Slovakia | With a foreword by Andrea Pető | ISBN 978-3-8382-1275-3

207 *Per A. Rudling* | Tarnished Heroes. The Organization of Ukrainian Nationalists in the Memory Politics of Post-Soviet Ukraine | ISBN 978-3-8382-0999-9

208 *Kaja Gadowska, Peter Solomon (Eds.)* | Legal Change in Post-Communist States. Progress, Reversions, Explanations | ISBN 978-3-8382-1312-5

209 *Paweł Kowal, Georges Mink, Iwona Reichardt (Eds.)* | Three Revolutions: Mobilization and Change in Contemporary Ukraine I. Theoretical Aspects and Analyses on Religion, Memory, and Identity | ISBN 978-3-8382-1321-7

210 *Paweł Kowal, Georges Mink, Adam Reichardt, Iwona Reichardt (Eds.)* | Three Revolutions: Mobilization and Change in Contemporary Ukraine II. An Oral History of the Revolution on Granite, Orange Revolution, and Revolution of Dignity | ISBN 978-3-8382-1323-1

211 *Li Bennich-Björkman, Sergiy Kurbatov (Eds.)* | When the Future Came. The Collapse of the USSR and the Emergence of National Memory in Post-Soviet History Textbooks | ISBN 978-3-8382-1335-4

212 *Olga R. Gulina* | Migration as a (Geo-)Political Challenge in the Post-Soviet Space. Border Regimes, Policy Choices, Visa Agendas | With a foreword by Nils Muižnieks | ISBN 978-3-8382-1338-5

213 *Sanna Turoma, Kaarina Aitamurto, Slobodanka Vladiv-Glover (Eds.)* | Religion, Expression, and Patriotism in Russia. Essays on Post-Soviet Society and the State. ISBN 978-3-8382-1346-0

214 *Vasif Huseynov* | Geopolitical Rivalries in the "Common Neighborhood". Russia's Conflict with the West, Soft Power, and Neoclassical Realism | With a foreword by Nicholas Ross Smith | ISBN 978-3-8382-1277-7

215 *Mikhail Suslov* | Geopolitical Imagination. Ideology and Utopia in Post-Soviet Russia | With a foreword by Mark Bassin | ISBN 978-3-8382-1361-3

216 *Alexander Etkind, Mikhail Minakov (Eds.)* | Ideology after Union. Political Doctrines, Discourses, and Debates in Post-Soviet Societies | ISBN 978-3-8382-1388-0

217 *Jakob Mischke, Oleksandr Zabirko (Hgg.)* | Protestbewegungen im langen Schatten des Kreml. Aufbruch und Resignation in Russland und der Ukraine | ISBN 978-3-8382-0926-5

218 *Oksana Huss* | How Corruption and Anti-Corruption Policies Sustain Hybrid Regimes. Strategies of Political Domination under Ukraine's Presidents in 1994-2014 | With a foreword by Tobias Debiel and Andrea Gawrich | ISBN 978-3-8382-1430-6

219 *Dmitry Travin, Vladimir Gel'man, Otar Marganiya* | The Russian Path. Ideas, Interests, Institutions, Illusions | With a foreword by Vladimir Ryzhkov | ISBN 978-3-8382-1421-4

220 *Gergana Dimova* | Political Uncertainty. A Comparative Exploration | With a foreword by Todor Yalamov and Rumena Filipova | ISBN 978-3-8382-1385-9

221 *Torben Waschke* | Russland in Transition. Geopolitik zwischen Raum, Identität und Machtinteressen | Mit einem Vorwort von Andreas Dittmann | ISBN 978-3-8382-1480-1

222 *Steven Jobbitt, Zsolt Bottlik, Marton Berki (Eds.)* | Power and Identity in the Post-Soviet Realm. Geographies of Ethnicity and Nationality after 1991 | ISBN 978-3-8382-1399-6

223 *Daria Buteiko* | Erinnerungsort. Ort des Gedenkens, der Erholung oder der Einkehr? Kommunismus-Erinnerung am Beispiel der Gedenkstätte Berliner Mauer sowie des Soloveckij-Klosters und -Museumsparks | ISBN 978-3-8382-1367-5

224 *Olga Bertelsen (Ed.)* | Russian Active Measures. Yesterday, Today, Tomorrow | With a foreword by Jan Goldman | ISBN 978-3-8382-1529-7

225 *David Mandel* | "Optimizing" Higher Education in Russia. University Teachers and their Union "Universitetskaya solidarnost'" | ISBN 978-3-8382-1519-8

226 *Mikhail Minakov, Gwendolyn Sasse, Daria Isachenko (Eds.)* | Post-Soviet Secessionism. Nation-Building and State-Failure after Communism | ISBN 978-3-8382-1538-9

227 *Jakob Hauter (Ed.)* | Civil War? Interstate War? Hybrid War? Dimensions and Interpretations of the Donbas Conflict in 2014–2020 | With a foreword by Andrew Wilson | ISBN 978-3-8382-1383-5

228 *Tima T. Moldogaziev, Gene A. Brewer, J. Edward Kellough (Eds.)* | Public Policy and Politics in Georgia. Lessons from Post-Soviet Transition | With a foreword by Dan Durning | ISBN 978-3-8382-1535-8

229 *Oxana Schmies (Ed.)* | NATO's Enlargement and Russia. A Strategic Challenge in the Past and Future | With a foreword by Vladimir Kara-Murza | ISBN 978-3-8382-1478-8

230 *Christopher Ford* | Ukapisme – Une Gauche perdue. Le marxisme anti-colonial dans la révolution ukrainienne 1917-1925 | Avec une préface de Vincent Présumey | ISBN 978-3-8382-0899-2

231 *Anna Kutkina* | Between Lenin and Bandera. Decommunization and Multivocality in Post-Euromaidan Ukraine | With a foreword by Juri Mykkänen | ISBN 978-3-8382-1506-8

232 *Lincoln E. Flake* | Defending the Faith. The Russian Orthodox Church and the Demise of Religious Pluralism | With a foreword by Peter Martland | ISBN 978-3-8382-1378-1

233 *Nikoloz Samkharadze* | Russia's Recognition of the Independence of Abkhazia and South Ossetia. Analysis of a Deviant Case in Moscow's Foreign Policy | With a foreword by Neil MacFarlane | ISBN 978-3-8382-1414-6

234 *Arve Hansen* | Urban Protest. A Spatial Perspective on Kyiv, Minsk, and Moscow | With a foreword by Julie Wilhelmsen | ISBN 978-3-8382-1495-5

235 *Eleonora Narvselius, Julie Fedor (Eds.)* | Diversity in the East-Central European Borderlands. Memories, Cityscapes, People | ISBN 978-3-8382-1523-5

236 *Regina Elsner* | The Russian Orthodox Church and Modernity. A Historical and Theological Investigation into Eastern Christianity between Unity and Plurality | With a foreword by Mikhail Suslov | ISBN 978-3-8382-1568-6

237 *Bo Petersson* | The Putin Predicament. Problems of Legitimacy and Succession in Russia | With a foreword by J. Paul Goode | ISBN 978-3-8382-1050-6

238 *Jonathan Otto Pohl* | The Years of Great Silence. The Deportation, Special Settlement, and Mobilization into the Labor Army of Ethnic Germans in the USSR, 1941–1955 | ISBN 978-3-8382-1630-0

239 *Mikhail Minakov (Ed.)* | Inventing Majorities. Ideological Creativity in Post-Soviet Societies | ISBN 978-3-8382-1641-6

240 *Robert M. Cutler* | Soviet and Post-Soviet Foreign Policies I. East-South Relations and the Political Economy of the Communist Bloc, 1971–1991 | With a foreword by Roger E. Kanet | ISBN 978-3-8382-1654-6

241 *Izabella Agardi* | On the Verge of History. Life Stories of Rural Women from Serbia, Romania, and Hungary, 1920–2020 | With a foreword by Andrea Pető | ISBN 978-3-8382-1602-7

242 *Sebastian Schäffer (Ed.)* | Ukraine in Central and Eastern Europe. Kyiv's Foreign Affairs and the International Relations of the Post-Communist Region | With a foreword by Pavlo Klimkin and Andreas Umland| ISBN 978-3-8382-1615-7

243 *Volodymyr Dubrovskyi, Kalman Mizsei, Mychailo Wynnyckyj (Eds.)* | Eight Years after the Revolution of Dignity. What Has Changed in Ukraine during 2013–2021? | With a foreword by Yaroslav Hrytsak | ISBN 978-3-8382-1560-0

244 *Rumena Filipova* | Constructing the Limits of Europe Identity and Foreign Policy in Poland, Bulgaria, and Russia since 1989 | With forewords by Harald Wydra and Gergana Yankova-Dimova | ISBN 978-3-8382-1649-2

245 *Oleksandra Keudel* | How Patronal Networks Shape Opportunities for Local Citizen Participation in a Hybrid Regime A Comparative Analysis of Five Cities in Ukraine | With a foreword by Sabine Kropp | ISBN 978-3-8382-1671-3

246 *Jan Claas Behrends, Thomas Lindenberger, Pavel Kolar (Eds.)* | Violence after Stalin Institutions, Practices, and Everyday Life in the Soviet Bloc 1953–1989 | ISBN 978-3-8382-1637-9

247 *Leonid Luks* | Macht und Ohnmacht der Utopien Essays zur Geschichte Russlands im 20. und 21. Jahrhundert | ISBN 978-3-8382-1677-5

248 *Iuliia Barshadska* | Brüssel zwischen Kyjiw und Moskau Das auswärtige Handeln der Europäischen Union im ukrainisch-russischen Konflikt 2014-2019 | Mit einem Vorwort von Olaf Leiße | ISBN 978-3-8382-1667-6

249 *Valentyna Romanova* | Decentralisation and Multilevel Elections in Ukraine Reform Dynamics and Party Politics in 2010–2021 | With a foreword by Kimitaka Matsuzato | ISBN 978-3-8382-1700-0

250 *Alexander Motyl* | National Questions. Theoretical Reflections on Nations and Nationalism in Eastern Europe | ISBN 978-3-8382-1675-1

251 *Marc Dietrich* | A Cosmopolitan Model for Peacebuilding. The Ukrainian Cases of Crimea and the Donbas | With a foreword by Rémi Baudouï | ISBN 978-3-8382-1687-4

252 *Eduard Baidaus* | An Unsettled Nation. Moldova in the Geopolitics of Russia, Romania, and Ukraine | With forewords by John-Paul Himka and David R. Marples | ISBN 978-3-8382-1582-2

253 *Igor Okunev, Petr Oskolkov (Eds.)* | Transforming the Administrative Matryoshka. The Reform of Autonomous Okrugs in the Russian Federation, 2003–2008 | With a foreword by Vladimir Zorin | ISBN 978-3-8382-1721-5

254 *Winfried Schneider-Deters* | Ukraine's Fateful Years 2013–2019. Vol. I: The Popular Uprising in Winter 2013/2014 | ISBN 978-3-8382-1725-3

255 *Winfried Schneider-Deters* | Ukraine's Fateful Years 2013–2019. Vol. II: The Annexation of Crimea and the War in Donbas | ISBN 978-3-8382-1726-0

256 *Robert M. Cutler* | Soviet and Post-Soviet Russian Foreign Policies II. East-West Relations in Europe and the Political Economy of the Communist Bloc, 1971–1991 | With a foreword by Roger E. Kanet | ISBN 978-3-8382-1727-7

257 *Robert M. Cutler* | Soviet and Post-Soviet Russian Foreign Policies III. East-West Relations in Europe and Eurasia in the Post-Cold War Transition, 1991–2001 | With a foreword by Roger E. Kanet | ISBN 978-3-8382-1728-4

258 *Paweł Kowal, Iwona Reichardt, Kateryna Pryshchepa (Eds.)* | Three Revolutions: Mobilization and Change in Contemporary Ukraine III. Archival Records and Historical Sources on the 1990 Revolution on Granite | ISBN 978-3-8382-1376-3

259 *Mikhail Minakov (Ed.)* | Philosophy Unchained. Developments in Post-Soviet Philosophical Thought. | With a foreword by Christopher Donohue | ISBN 978-3-8382-1768-0

260 *David Dalton* | The Ukrainian Oligarchy After the Euromaidan. How Ukraine's Political Economy Regime Survived the Crisis | With a foreword by Andrew Wilson | ISBN 978-3-8382-1740-6

261 *Andreas Heinemann-Grüder (Ed.)* | Who Are the Fighters? Irregular Armed Groups in the Russian-Ukrainian War since 2014 | ISBN 978-3-8382-1777-2

262 *Taras Kuzio (Ed.)* | Russian Disinformation and Western Scholarship. Bias and Prejudice in Journalistic, Expert, and Academic Analyses of East European, Russian and Eurasian Affairs | ISBN 978-3-8382-1685-0

263 *Darius Furmonavicius* | LithuaniaTransforms the West. Lithuania's Liberation from Soviet Occupation and the Enlargement of NATO (1988–2022) | With a foreword by Vytautas Landsbergis | ISBN 978-3-8382-1779-6

264 *Dirk Dalberg* | Politisches Denken im tschechoslowakischen Dissens. Egon Bondy, Miroslav Kusý, Milan Šimečka und Petr Uhl (1968-1989) | ISBN 978-3-8382-1318-7

265 *Леонид Люкс* | К столетию «философского парохода». Мыслители «первой» русской эмиграции о русской революции и о тоталитарных соблазнах XX века | ISBN 978-3-8382-1775-8

266 *Daviti Mtchedlishvili* | The EU and the South Caucasus. European Neighborhood Policies between Eclecticism and Pragmatism, 1991-2021 | With a foreword by Nicholas Ross Smith | ISBN 978-3-8382-1735-2

267 *Bohdan Harasymiw* | Post-Euromaidan Ukraine. Domestic Power Struggles and War of National Survival in 2014–2022 | ISBN 978-3-8382-1798-7

268 *Nadiia Koval, Denys Tereshchenko (Eds.)* | Russian Cultural Diplomacy under Putin. Rossotrudnichestvo, the "Russkiy Mir" Foundation, and the Gorchakov Fund in 2007–2022 | ISBN 978-3-8382-1801-4

269 *Izabela Kazejak* | Jews in Post-War Wrocław and L'viv. Official Policies and Local Responses in Comparative Perspective, 1945-1970s | ISBN 978-3-8382-1802-1

270 *Jakob Hauter* | Russia's Overlooked Invasion. The Causes of the 2014 Outbreak of War in Ukraine's Donbas | With a foreword by Hiroaki Kuromiya | ISBN 978-3-8382-1803-8

271 *Anton Shekhovtsov* | Russian Political Warfare. Essays on Kremlin Propaganda in Europe and the Neighbourhood, 2020-2023 | With a foreword by Nathalie Loiseau | ISBN 978-3-8382-1821-2

272 *Андреа Пето* | Насилие и Молчание. Красная армия в Венгрии во Второй Мировой войне | ISBN 978-3-8382-1636-2

273 *Winfried Schneider-Deters* | Russia's War in Ukraine. Debates on Peace, Fascism, and War Crimes, 2022–2023 | With a foreword by Klaus Gestwa | ISBN 978-3-8382-1876-2

274 *Rasmus Nilsson* | Uncanny Allies. Russia and Belarus on the Edge, 2012-2024 | ISBN 978-3-8382-1288-3

275 *Anton Grushetskyi, Volodymyr Paniotto* | War and the Transformation of Ukrainian Society (2022–23). Empirical Evidence | ISBN 978-3-8382-1944-8

276 *Christian Kaunert, Alex MacKenzie, Adrien Nonjon (Eds.)* | In the Eye of the Storm. Origins, Ideology, and Controversies of the Azov Brigade, 2014–23 | ISBN 978-3-8382-1750-5

277 *Gian Marco Moisé* | The House Always Wins. The Corrupt Strategies that Shaped Kazakh Oil Politics and Business in the Nazarbayev Era | With a foreword by Alena Ledeneva | ISBN 978-3-8382-1917-2

278 *Mikhail Minakov* | The Post-Soviet Human. Philosophical Reflections on Social History after the End of Communism | ISBN 978-3-8382-1943-1

279 *Natalia Kudriavtseva, Debra A. Friedman (Eds.)* | Language and Power in Ukraine and Kazakhstan. Essays on Education, Ideology, Literature, Practice, and the Media | With a foreword by Laada Bilaniuk | ISBN 978-3-8382-1949-3

280 *Georges Mink, Iwona Reichardt (Eds.)* | The End of the Soviet World? Essays on Post-Communist Political and Social Change | With an afterword by Richardt Butterwick | ISBN 978-3-8382-1961-5

281 *Kateryna Zarembo, Michèle Knodt, Maksym Yakovlyev (Eds.)* | Teaching IR in Wartime. Experiences of University Lecturers during Russia's Full-Scale Invasion of Ukraine | ISBN 978-3-8382-1954-7

282 *Oleksiy V. Kresin* | The United Nations General Assembly Resolutions. Their Nature and Significance in the Context of the Russian War Against Ukraine | Edited by William E. Butler | ISBN 978-3-8382-1967-7

283 *Jakob Hauter* | Russlands unbemerkte Invasion. Die Ursachen des Kriegsausbruchs im ukrainischen Donbas im Jahr 2014 | Mit einem Vorwort von Hiroaki Kuromiya | ISBN 978-3-8382-2003-1

284 „Alles kann sich ändern". Letzte Worte politisch Angeklagter vor Gericht in Russland | Herausgegeben von Memorial Deutschland e.V. | ISBN 978-3-8382-1994-3

285 *Nadiya Kiss, Monika Wingender (Eds.)* | Contested Language Diversity in Wartime Ukraine. National Minorities, Language Biographies, and Linguistic Landscape | ISBN 978-3-8382-1966-0

286 *Richard Ottinger (Ed.)* | Religious Elements in the Russian War of Aggression Against Ukraine. Propaganda, Religious Politics and Pastoral Care, 2014–2024 | ISBN 978-3-8382-1981-3

287 *Yuri Radchenko* | Helping in Mass Murders. Auxiliary Police, Indigenous Administration, SD, and the Shoa in the Ukrainian-Russian-Belorussian Borderlands, 1941–43 | With forewords by John-Paul Himka and Kai Struve | ISBN 978-3-8382-1878-6

288 *Zsofia Maria Schmidt* | Hungary's System of National Cooperation. Strategies of Framing in Pro-Governmental Media and Public Discourse, 2010–18 | With a foreword by Andreas Schmidt-Schweizer | ISBN 978-3-8382-1983-7

289 *Richard Ottinger (Hrsg.)* | Religiöse Elemente im russischen Angriffskrieg gegen die Ukraine. Propaganda, Religionspolitik und Seelsorge, 2014–2024 | ISBN 978-3-8382-1980-6

290 Galyna Zelenko (Ed.) | Crises of Political Development in Ukraine. The Challenges of Post-Soviet State-Building and Ways to Overcome Them | With a foreword by Oleg Rafalskiy | ISBN 978-3-8382-2027-7

291 Galyna Zelenko (Ed.) | Fake Russia. Investigations into Moscow's Imitations of Greatness and Power | ISBN 978-3-8382-1997-4

292 Ian Garner, Taras Kuzio (Eds.) | Russia and Modern Fascism. New Perspectives on the Kremlin's War Against Ukraine | With a foreword by David Satter | ISBN 978-3-8382-2015-4

293 Tatyana Shchyttsova | Solidarity of the Shaken. On the Collective Subject of the Belarusian Revolution of 2020 | ISBN 978-3-8382-2030-7

294 Andrii Martynov | Imagining Europe and Ukraine. Mutual Perceptions of Europeans and Ukrainians in the 20th and Early 21st Century | With a foreword by Eduard Afonin | ISBN 978-3-8382-2037-6

295 Felix Riefer, Julie Fedor, Leonid Luks, and Andreas Umland (Eds.) | Russia Before the Full-Scale War. Vol. I: Elites, Institutions, and Society, 1991–2021 | ISBN 978-3-8382-1935-6

296 Felix Riefer, Julie Fedor, Leonid Luks, and Andreas Umland (Eds.) | Russia Before the Full-Scale War. Vol. II: Memories, Ideologies and Politics, 1991–2021 | ISBN 978-3-8382-2045-1

297 Leonid Luks | Aggrieved Powers? Essays on Contemporary Russian and German History | ISBN 978-3-8382-2075-8

ibidem.eu